Celestial
Navigation

...fe

fernhurst
B O O K S

www.fernhurstbooks.co.uk

© Fernhurst Books 2001

Second edition published in 2001 by
Fernhurst Books,
Duke's Path, High Street, Arundel,
West Sussex, BN18 9AJ, England

First edition © 1989

British Library Cataloguing in Publication Data.
A catalogue record for this book is available
from the British Library

ISBN 1 898660 75 1

Printed in Hong Kong
through World Print.

Acknowledgements

The author and publisher would like to thank
Bill Anderson of the RYA for his advice on the
manuscript. The tables on pages 30-39 have been
reproduced from The Nautical Almanac and
Sight Reduction Tables for Air Navigation (AP
3270) Volumes 1 and 3, with permission from
data supplied by HM Nautical Almanac Office,
copyright Council for the Central Laboratory of
the Research Councils.

Photographs

The photographs on the pages indicated were
supplied by the following individuals or
agencies. All others by Tom Cunliffe.
Particle Physics & Asronomy Research Council 45,
Cover photo courtesy of Vega Instruments
(distributors of fine sextants).

Edited by Rosalind Byrne
Artwork by Creative Byte
Cover design by Simon Balley

For a free, full-colour brochure write,
phone, fax or email us:

Fernhurst Books, Duke's Path,
High Street, Arundel, West Sussex
BN18 9AJ, United Kingdom
Phone: 01903 882277
Fax: 01903 882715
email: sales@fernhurstbooks.co.uk

Contents

Foreword

For a thousand years, celestial navigation in one form or another has guided mariners across the trackless oceans, and since the days of Captain Cook a seaman has needed only two mechanical devices to ascertain his position to within a mile or two: a sextant and a chronometer, given a decent horizon and a glimpse of the heavens.

Only the most cynical of navigators has not at some time looked at the fix on his chart in awe, remembering that the position lines have been derived from stars and galaxies marching at unimaginable distances through space. Whilst the electronics of the late twentieth century can only stand to increase man's pride in his own works, the celestial navigation of the ages encourages a deep humility which, at sea in a small vessel, is no bad thing.

At the time of its early editions, this book held the only key to fixing a position off soundings. Today, 'astro' has become a secondary system, a back-up for when the rest goes wrong. This perspective is not only a tragedy for the seaman's understanding of his place in the universe, it also leads to the dangerous but natural practice of ignoring celestial navigation until it is really needed. Like all arts, sextant work requires continuous effort to approach a reasonable standard. Just buying the book and the instrument isn't enough.

The author can testify to the tremendous job satisfaction achieved by crossing an ocean with no other guides but a compass and the signs of heaven. You need no more than these, but since even the most careful of us could one day drop the sextant over the side, or smash the deck

watch with a winch handle intended for a mutineer, it makes sense to invest in a GPS to back up your sun sights. Bear in mind, though, that the firmament will continue to blaze long after the last navigational satellite has escaped into deep space, or burned up in the final truth of its re-entry.

This little book has been written to enable an offshore yacht skipper to enter the exclusive world of those able to navigate by Sun, Moon and stars. The material is organised so as to get you going long before you have finished reading, but this does not mean that everything after the early 'sun' chapters is unimportant. The reason why the sun is placed 'up front' is that it is the easiest of all the heavenly bodies to shoot and it can be used for a 'stand-alone' system based on running fixes. For a one-off single fix it is still impossible to beat twilight stars and a planet or two. Stars are surprisingly easy to work, the planets are a delight to identify and as easy as the sun to reduce, while even the Moon can be valuable as it peers quizzically over your shoulder.

I have never been good at sums and I didn't do too well on my astro night-school course. I have learned celestial navigation at sea and been amazed at how simple it can be, but you do have to master some elementary theory to make sense of it all. If you try to skip the concepts and definitions of Chapter 1 you may as well have left the book on the rack. So persevere. Once the conventions are on board, the rest of the subject should be a source of almost mystical joy.

Introduction

*NAVIGATION is that art which instructs
the mariner in what manner to conduct
a ship through the wide and trackless ocean,
from one part to another,
with the greatest safety, and in the
shortest time possible.*

*J W Norie
Norie's Practical Navigation
(mid-nineteenth century)*

Ocean navigation has changed utterly in the twenty-five years between my first venture across the Atlantic as skipper and my most recent crossing of the same stretch of water. From celestial navigation as the only option, we have stumbled through a dawn period of transit satellites into the full daylight of universal GPS. If the bulkhead GPS fails for any reason out on the wide ocean, the skipper simply reaches into his kitbag for the backup unit he bought at the boat show for the price of his night's lodging. Those whose experience of technology has presented a catalogue of disappointment may even have invested in more than two such wonders.

Since the beginnings of seafaring, mankind has navigated under the inescapable reality that for much of the time his position was seen through a frosted window. All at once, technology has leapt ahead, and an exact fix is available whenever we desire it. For the foreseeable future, therefore, mainstream navigators will use GPS as their primary fixing tool. Celestial navigation is deposed from its hitherto unassailable situation at the summit of the navigator's achievement. Overnight, the

skills of the ages have been degraded to mere back-up against the ultimate catastrophe, loss of volts. For many sailors, however, the change is to be lamented as well as welcomed.

Until a few years ago, you would have plunged into the Celestial Navigation section of the Yachtmaster Ocean syllabus in earnest, for without it, you would have been truly lost while off soundings. Except in emergency, this is no longer the case, but it does not mean that when things are going smoothly on the electronic front the old ways should be consigned to an unvisited corner of the mind.

First, there is a spiritual aspect to the regular use of the sextant. Only the most cynical never felt a tingle of pure awe at the thought that they had fixed their position to within a mile or two on the planet we call home by observations of stars and galaxies marching in silence through the infinity of space. This daily connection with the heavens used to serve as a constant reminder of our own ultimate insignificance - no bad thing for a seaman, or anyone else for that matter. Together with this metaphysical aspect to astro-navigation came a constant uncertainty about one's position which bred seamanlike caution. When finally dispelled by a good landfall, this gave rise to an elation that no longer has a parallel. All this is potentially lost to the electronic navigator.

Of greater concern to some, however, will be that sextant work, like all arts, requires continuous practice to achieve any real proficiency. Buying the book and the instrument isn't enough. Nor is it sufficient to take a couple of sun sights on a long passage and send them to an examiner who may then declare you an Ocean Yachtmaster. The traditional daily round of morning or evening stars and the forenoon sight of the sun followed by a noon latitude not only gave rhythm to the watch system, it also bred a facility with the tools that today's navigator will still need if the magic box ever goes down.

For all these reasons, any skipper of a yacht on the ocean should make the effort to master celestial navigation. The methods and techniques have been set out here in a form that will get you navigating by the sky as soon as possible - long before you have finished the book - but do not for one moment suppose that because the Sun makes its appearance in these pages before the stars that it is more important. You have to start somewhere and the Sun is pretty hard to miss, so it's the best thing on which to practise using your sextant. It won't help you much though, if you are expecting a dawn landfall on an unlit coast and you are wondering where you are, because it won't be around to be observed until after breakfast. Instead, morning stars and a planet or two thrown in for good measure will, if the sky is clear, fix your position to within a mile or so. As you will see, stars are surprisingly easy to operate with, the planets are a delight to identify and simple to reduce, and even the Moon, smiling wryly down on our efforts, can provide a useful signpost.

I am not an astronomer. I am by no stretch of the imagination either a physicist or a mathematician. I am, before everything, a practical seaman. I have learned navigation the easy way, by spending long periods of time at sea. One by one I have forced myself over the hurdles presented in my mind by planets, Moon and stars and found on each occasion that what I imagined to be a problem soluble only by the academic or hard-line professional turned out to be yet another piece of cake.

The whole business, if tackled in the right order, is amazingly simple. In the following chapters I have set out from my own experience what you need to know. Very little more, and no less. You'll notice that Chapter 1 is all about concepts, conventions and definitions. `In the beginning was The Word'. Skip it, and you're in trouble. Read it, understand it and be ready to refer back to it because it is the rock on which the rest is built. Once you're over Chapter 1, which should be interesting if only for the new perspective on your surroundings, the rest of the book will be pure joy. So welcome to the World of the Enlightened. Fair winds to you on your voyage!

1 The Earth and the heavens

At school we all learn that the Earth revolves once a day and that the stars remain, to a greater or lesser extent, stationary. We also learn that the Moon is in our own back yard, that the stars are plunging through space at various mind-boggling distances from us and that the Earth is travelling on a annual voyage around the Sun. Whether or not all this is true is of no relevance to the practical astro-navigator. For our purposes the Earth, otherwise known as the *terrestrial sphere*, is a perfectly round ball swimming in a vacuum at the centre of the known universe.

At the outside of the vacuum, an indeterminate but fortunately irrelevant distance away, is the big ball which marks the perimeter of the universe. This ball is known as the *celestial sphere*. For our purposes all the heavenly bodies move in their courses on its inside surface, and its centre coincides exactly with the centre of the Earth.

THE TERRESTRIAL SPHERE

Any location on the Earth's surface can be expressed in terms of latitude and longitude.

Meridians of longitude

To define our position on the globe in an east-west direction we make use of the meridians of longitude. These, you will recall, are great circles which converge at the poles of the Earth, a great circle being the line described on the Earth's surface by a plane passing through the centre of the Earth. Any great circle must have equal halves in the northern and southern hemispheres, and its points of greatest latitude are called its *Vertices* (singular, *Vertex*). At the vertex, it is making a tangent to the adjacent parallel of latitude and is thus travelling briefly east-west.

We measure our position in terms of *angular distance* east or west of the zero° or datum meridian. This passes through the Greenwich Observatory in England, and is therefore known as the *Greenwich Meridian*.

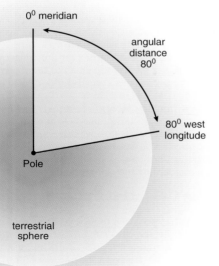

Looking down on the Earth's axis from the Pole.
An observer at 80⁰W longitude is at an angular distance of 80⁰ west of the Greenwich Meridian.

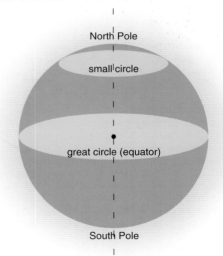

Great and small circles (Earth viewed from just north of the equator). *The equator is a great circle - that is, on a plane that passes through the centre of the Earth - but all the other parallels of latitude are small circles.*

Parallels of latitude

Having determined our angular distance east or west of Greenwich we need another set of co-ordinates to fix us in a north/south direction. These are the parallels of latitude, which define our angular distance north or south of the *equator*, which is the great circle on a plane at right angles to the Earth's axis, halfway between two poles.

The equator is the only parallel of latitude which fulfils the definition of a great circle. All the others are *small circles* (see diagram).

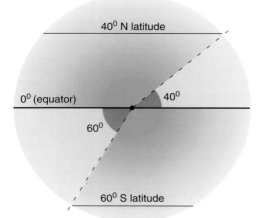

Latitude - the Earth (the terrestrial sphere) viewed from the plane of the equator. *Latitude is expressed as an angular distance north or south of the equator, measured from the centre of the Earth.*

Geographic position

Any point on the Earth's surface fixed by its *terrestrial co-ordinates* (latitude and longitude), is known as a *geographic position* (GP).

Angular distance

Distances between locations on Earth are generally expressed in miles or kilometres. This is convenient because we need to time our journeys. But for the purposes of celestial navigation the most convenient unit of distance is a degree of the 360° circle. It would be impossible to try to handle the north/south distance between Sirius and Aldebaran in terms of miles, but to say that it is 33° measured from the centre of the Earth is quite comprehensible and very easy to work with.

Subdivision of degrees

A degree subdivides into 60 minutes (60'), and each minute into 60 seconds (60"). By a wonderful coincidence (or is it?) one minute of

The celestial sphere is an imaginary sphere enclosing the Earth, with its own poles and equator. *For the purposes of navigation, all celestial bodies such as the Sun and the stars are positioned on the surface of this sphere regardless of their actual distance fron the Earth.*

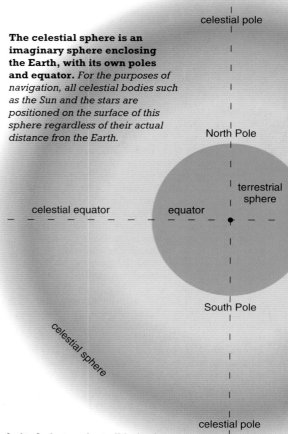

latitude is equal, at all latitudes, to one nautical mile (1M). One second of latitude is equal to 101 feet, or three boat lengths for the average yacht. Since this is clearly too small to be of any serious use, minutes of arc are subdivided into decimal points, thus: 36° 14.1' N.

One minute of longitude equals one mile at the equator, but diminishes to zero at the poles. Working out what it represents in between in terms of miles would mean yet another sum, so there, straight away, is a very good reason for the concept of angular distance.

The Celestial Sphere

Just as it is possible to fix a position on the Earth's surface using its terrestrial co-ordinates of latitude and longitude, so the exact situation of a heavenly body on the surface of the celestial sphere can be defined by its *celestial co-ordinates*.

All the main features of the terrestrial sphere are mirrored in its celestial counterpart.

The terrestrial poles, if projected outwards from the centre of the Earth onto the celestial sphere, form the *celestial poles*. The terrestrial equator is projected outwards to throw a 'great circle' onto the celestial sphere equidistant at all points from the celestial poles. This is called the *celestial equator*.

Celestial longitude
- or Greenwich Hour Angle (GHA)

Since the first edition of this book, the notion of Greenwich Mean Time (GMT) has been replaced by Universal Time (UT). You may well find that modern almanacs and data in general refer to UT. The tables here refer to GMT for publishing convenience. There is no practical difference between the two.

The *celestial zero meridian* is the projection of the terrestrial zero (Greenwich) meridian. However, whereas terrestrial longitude is measured from the Greenwich meridian in degrees *east* or *west* around the world to 180° on the opposite side, celestial longitude, which is known as Greenwich Hour Angle (GHA), is measured to the westward **only** in degrees from 0° to 360°. When considering matters concerning the concept of Greenwich Hour Angle, never forget that it is merely a way of expressing celestial longitude.

You will see in the diagram below that 40°W longitude is the equivalent of a GHA of 40° on the celestial sphere, and that 120° E longitude marries up with GHA 240°. A second glance will show that if 120°E were expressed in a 0° to 360° notation, beginning at Greenwich and working westward, it would represent a longitude of 240°. It is just a question of convention and, for better or worse, longitude is expressed as 0° to 180° east or west, and GHA as 0° to 360°.

To convert east longitude to 360° notation and tie it in with the corresponding GHA, simply subtract the figure from 360°. Thus 120° east is equivalent to a GHA of 360 minus 120, or 240°.

To find the GHA of a body for a given time (and it changes by the second as the Earth turns) you need to consult the daily pages of *The Nautical Almanac*. Illustrated on pages 30-31 is the pair of daily pages for 1st, 2nd and 3rd of May 1986. You will see that on the right-hand page the far left column refers to hours of GMT and the next column gives the GHA of the Sun for the hour *exactly*. To find the increment by which it varies for minutes and seconds of time, you turn to the 'increments' tables in the back pages of the almanac, an example of which is illustrated on page 32, and read off the answer, making sure that you take it from the correct column.

Note that since the heavenly bodies are moving westward, their GHA goes on increasing until it reads 360°, when it starts again. This means that you always *add* the minutes and seconds increment to the hourly value of the GHA.

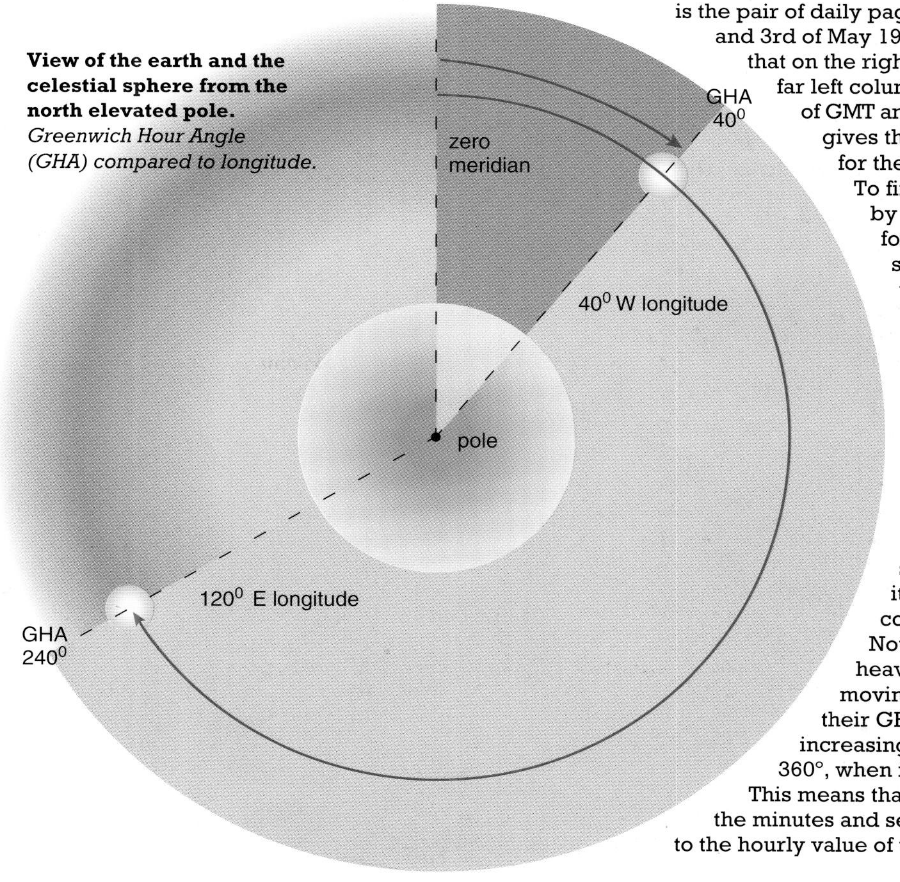

View of the earth and the celestial sphere from the north elevated pole.
Greenwich Hour Angle (GHA) compared to longitude.

Example

What is the GHA of the Sun at 10h 15m 47s GMT on May 1st 1986?

GHA 10h	330° 43′	.5
+ Increment for 15m 47s	3° 56′	.8
GHA Sun	334° 40′	.3

Notice that 43′.5 + 56′.8 equals 1° 40′.3. You only have to get to 60 minutes to make one degree.

Celestial latitude, or declination

The cross co-ordinate used on the celestial sphere to fix the position of a heavenly body north or south on its GHA co-ordinate is its *declination*. As you will by now be able to predict, it corresponds exactly to terrestrial latitude.

Declination is actually angular distance north or south of the celestial equator and, like terrestrial latitude, it is conveniently named north or south.

A body with a *declination* of 42°N will, at some time in the 24-hour period, pass directly over the head of an observer in 42°N latitude.

To calculate the declination of a body for a given time you need once more to consult the almanac.

Look again at the daily pages illustration (pages 30-31) and notice that each column gives not only the changing GHA of the body, but also its declination.

At the bottom of the column is a small letter 'd' with a numerical value beside it. This is the rate of change per hour. Inspection of the hours adjacent to the one you are interested in will show whether the change is to be added or subtracted, depending on whether declination is increasing or decreasing.

If you look now at the illustration of the 'increments' page (page 32), you will see a column for each minute headed 'v' or 'd' correction.

Suppose you are interested in a 14-minute increment and a 'd' value of + 0.9. You go down the column for 14 minutes until you come to 'd' 0.9 and read off the value, which is + 0.2. It is this figure that you add to the hourly declination figure you have taken from the daily page. Notice that 'v' and 'd' corrections do not refer to seconds of time. The figures in the column are for minutes only, which is invariably quite accurate enough.

In practice, you can usually work out the declination for a given number of minutes after the hour by inspection and mental arithmetic, so recourse to the increment pages for changing declination is rare.

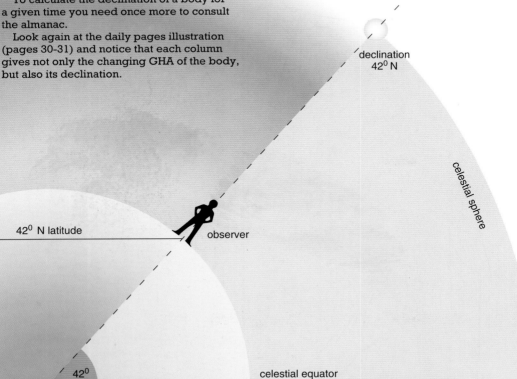

Earth and the celestial sphere from the equator. Latitude compared to declination.

In the case of the Moon, however, declination varies rapidly and hugely and the mental arithmetic involved in bypassing the 'd' increment is way beyond me. Here, then, is an example of its use:

Example

What is the declination of the Moon at 2314 on 3rd May 1986?

Dec 23h	S 8° 15′	.3
-d(14.4) 14m	3′	.5
Dec 2314	S 8° 11′	.8

Note that in this case 'd' is negative because declination is decreasing, and that the declination is always labelled N or S.

Zenith

An observer's *zenith* is his terrestrial position projected (from the centre of the Earth) onto the celestial sphere. In other words, the point directly above his head. The declination of his zenith is the same as his latitude. The GHA of his zenith is the same as his longitude. (Although in east longitude it will be necessary to adjust the longitude figure to read 0° to 360° notation by subtracting it from 360°.)

Opposite the observer's zenith is the celestial position delightfully termed his *nadir*. Project a line from his zenith through the observer to the centre of the Earth, keep going until you hit the celestial sphere on the other side, and you have it. As the name suggests, it's about as low as you can get.

Local Hour Angle

In the majority of the calculations involved in celestial nagivation you will need to use not the Greenwich Hour Angle of the body concerned, but the *Local Hour Angle* (LHA).

Just as the GHA of the body at a given time

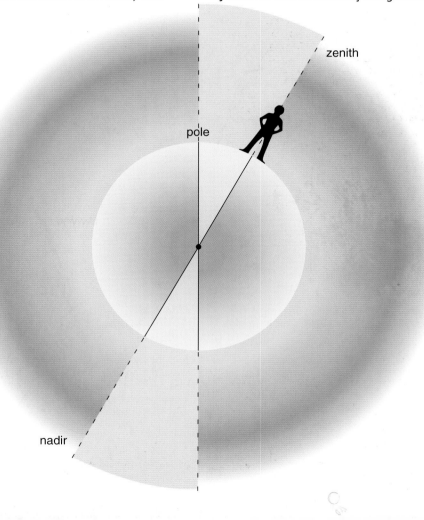

is its angular distance west of the *Greenwich* meridian, so the LHA of the same body is its angular distance to the west of the *observer's* meridian.

Given that you have extracted the GHA of the body from the almanac (see page 9) and you have some idea of your longitude, you should have no difficulty in working out the body's approximate LHA.

As always with angular questions, when in doubt draw a diagram. Below are four examples with diagrams to illustrate the four most likely calculations of LHA. They are quite simple and it is vital that they are understood. Without a grasp of the concept of Local Hour Angle, the rest of the book may as well be written in Hottentot for all the good it will do you.

Case 1

West longitude: GHA of Sun greater than observer's longitude.
In this case
LHA = GHA minus longitude west.

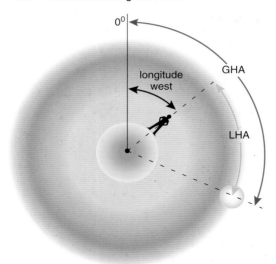

Example What is the LHA of the Sun at 16h 15m 27s GMT on 1st May 1986? Your longitude is 15° 23′W.

GHA 16h	60°	43′	.9
+ Increment 15m 27s	3°	51′	.8
GHA Sun	64°	35′	.7
—Longitude west	15°	23′	.0
LHA	49°	12′	.7

Case 2

West Longitude: GHA less than observer's longitude
If you study the diagram, you'll see that the logical answer in this case is to find the difference between the longitude west and the GHA and then subtract it from 360 (the remainder of the full circle).

On the face of it, this looks a bit awkward. By far the easiest way to handle it is to add the GHA to 360 and then subtract the west longitude. The answer comes out right every time.

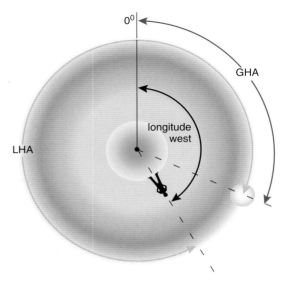

Example What is the LHA of the Sun at 14h 16m 18s GMT on Tuesday 3rd May 1986? Your longitude is 40° 13′W.

GHA 14h	30°	47′	.2
+ Increment 16m 18s	4°	04′	.5
GHA Sun	34°	51′	.7
+ 360	360°		
GHA + 360	394°	51′	.7
-Longitude west	40°	13′	.0
LHA	354°	38′	.7

In both examples, LHA = GHA minus longitude west. If longitude west happens to be greater than LHA and makes the sum a nonsense, just remember to add a quick 360° where it counts and all will be well.

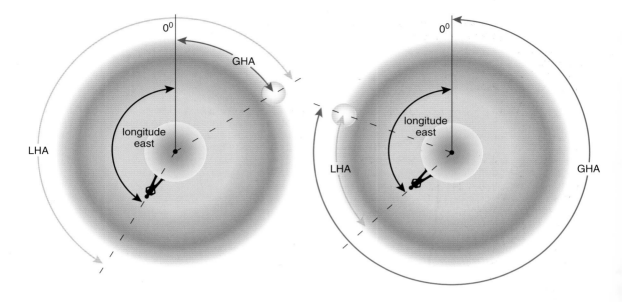

Case 3

East longitude: GHA a smaller value than the longitude (expressed in 360° notation).
A glance at the diagram makes this one obvious, remembering always that LHA is the angular distance of the body from the observer, moving to the westward (clockwise on the diagram). In this case LHA = GHA + longitude east.

Example What is the LHA of the Sun at 03h 15m 22s on May 1st 1986? Your longitude is 110°E.

GHA 03h	225°	42′	.9
+ Increment 15m 22s	3°	50′	.5
GHA Sun	229°	33′	.4
+ Longitude east	110°		
LHA Sun	339°	33′	.4

Case 4

East longitude: GHA a greater value than longitude (expressed in 360° notation).

This case is easier than a first glance at the diagram might suggest. You are looking for the angular distance to the westward between the observer and the Sun or star. One way to do this is to work your longitude into 360° notation and subtract it from the GHA, but the easiest way is to add up the GHA and the longitude expressed conventionally as degrees east (of Greenwich). The sum of the two will be greater than 360° which is a nonsense, but if you subtract 360° from the result, you will have the right answer.

Example What is the LHA of the Sun at 02h 17m 28s on May 3rd 1986? Your longitude is 172° 15′E.

GHA 02h	210°	46′	.4
+ Increment 17m 28s	4°	22′	.0
GHA Sun	215°	08′	.4
+ Longitude east	172°	15′	.0
	387°	23′	.4
—360	360°		
LHA Sun	27°	23′	.4

General rules

From the above examples you'll see that two general rules are applicable when working out LHA.

If you are in west longitude **LHA = GHA minus longitude west**. If GHA is a smaller figure than longitude west, just add 360° to it and carry on. It's as simple as that.
If you are in east longitude **LHA = GHA plus longitude east**. If the answer turns out to be greater than 360°, subtract 360° from it and there is the LHA.

Got it? Good, then carry on.

HORIZON

One final concept. Every schoolchild knows what the horizon is. Or thinks he does. There's just a bit more to it than that for the navigator. All astro-navigation depends upon observing

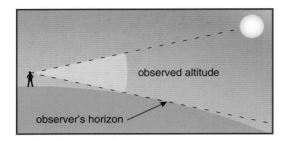

the 'altitudes' of the Sun, Moon, stars and planets. The altitudes are measured with a sextant and can only be observed as the angle at the observer between the heavenly body and the observer's horizon.

All the navigational tables work on the assumption that the observer with his sextant is at the centre of the terrestrial sphere, and not on the Earth's surface.

Because the Earth has a measurable size, at least in comparison with the distance to the Moon, the Sun and some of the planets, this discrepancy leads to an error of parallax between what he is actually seeing (the terrestrial or 'corrected' visual horizon) and what the tables want him to see (the celestial horizon).

This error is called *horizontal parallax*. It can be as much as one degree in the case of the Moon, which in consequence requires its own correction table, but it reduces to a fraction of

a minute for the Sun and the planets and, as you will see, is very easily dealt with.

The size of the Earth when related to the distance to the nearest star is a pitiful irrelevance so, when working up starsights, parallax is non-existent.

For purposes of calculation, what we are after is the angle (measured at the centre of the Earth) between the celestial horizon and the altitude of the Sun, Moon, star or planet.

The *celestial horizon* is on a plane constructed at right angles to a vertical line dropped from the position of the observer to the centre of the Earth.

The observer cannot see this horizon. What he can see (with a few small adjustments) is the *terrestrial horizon*. This is a plane drawn as a tangent to the Earth's surface and is at right angles to the line joining the observer, his zenith and the centre of the Earth.

Because the observer's eye will be above the surface of the Earth by anything from six feet in a small yacht to a hundred in a large tanker he is obviously going to see 'over the edge' and beyond the terrestrial horizon to his *visual horizon*. The angular inaccuracy thus caused is called *dip* and is taken care of by a small angular corrective factor given in the almanac.

Don't get concerned about horizons and parallax. In practice they present no difficulties at all.

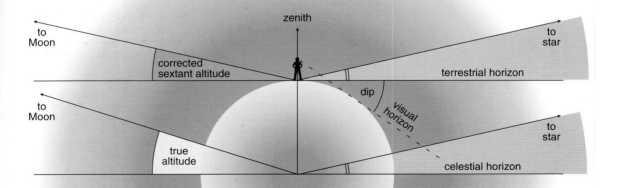

Owing to the close proximity of the Moon, there is a difference between its corrected sextant altitude and its true altitude from the centre of the Earth. Stars, on the other hand, are so far away that the sextant altitude and true altitude are effectively the same.

2 The sextant

In the last chapter I let slip that all astro-navigation depends upon observing the angle between the horizon and the heavenly body of your choice. Methods of achieving this measurement have improved no end over the years. The tenth-century Vikings, including Bjarni Herjolfsson, the discoverer of America, used to measure the altitude of Polaris using a notched stick. This gave them a crude comparative latitude without involving them in discussions about whether or not the world was round.

Today we have the sextant. It is so called because its calibrated arc is one-sixth of a circle, or 60°. By the doubling effect of its mirrors it is actually able to measure angles of up to 120°. This represents a big leap forward from its predecessor the octant, which has an arc of one-eighth of a circle, doubles up to only 90° and has thus been retired from active service to languish in picturesque obscurity on pub walls.

HOW THE SEXTANT WORKS

If you look at the sextant illustrated, or better still hold yours in your hand, you will see that

The tool of the trade: the sextant. You don't have to buy one like this - you can get cheap plastic ones that work very well, although they may need adjusting more often.

it consists of a frame with a handle, a moving 'index arm' with a mirror at one end and a micrometer at the other, and a fixed mirror upon which the telescope appears to focus.

Look more closely at the fixed mirror and you will see that it consists of two halves. One half is mirror, and the other is clear glass. That is the

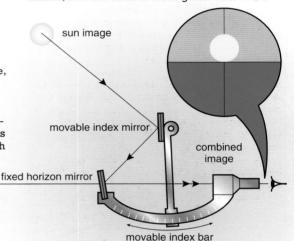

The index bar of the sextant is slid along the arc until the index mirror reflects the Sun's image onto the horizon mirror. When the two images coincide as shown, the reading on the arc represents the sextant altitude of the Sun.

secret of the instrument. Light from the heavenly body is reflected by the index mirror down onto the horizon mirror, which reflects it through the telescope to your eye. If the instrument is set up so that you are seeing the horizon through the plain glass with the reflected image of the heavenly body apparently 'sitting' on it, the sextant will tell you the angle between them.

SETTING UP THE SEXTANT

The first thing to do when you buy a sextant is to splice a lanyard to it to go around your neck. The next thing is to remove the telescope, focus it on infinity (the horizon) to suit your good eye, and then replace it.

Once you can see through the device properly you can *adjust* it to remove the various errors. These are as follows:

Perpendicularity

Effect: Images side by side.

Cause: Index and horizon mirrors out of parallel.

Cure: You need to adjust the index mirror. Look across the sextant so that you can see the image of the arc in the index mirror adjacent to the actual arc, as shown in the illustration. To arrange this you'll have to set the index bar to something like 60°. If the real arc will not run perfectly into its image without a 'step', this shows that there is an error of perpendicularity. You can remove it by adjusting the screw in the back of the index mirror with the tool provided. The index mirror is now 'true'.

Side error.
If you can place the images one on top of the other like this then there is no side error in the sextant.

Index error.
The sextant is set at zero, but despite this there is a step in the horizon line, indicating an index error. To deal with this, adjust the vertical alignment screw on the horizon mirror, checking the effect by sighting on the horizon line (below).

Perpendicularity. *This sextant has an error of perpendicularity, shown by the reflection of the arc in the index mirror (centre of top picture). The cure for this is to adjust the mirror (centre picture) until the arc and its reflection run into each other without a step (lower picture).*

Side error (see left)

Effect: Images side by side.
Cause: Since the index mirror is now 'proved',
the error must lie in the horizon mirror.
Cure: First set the instrument to zero. The
horizon mirror has two adjusting screws.
To take out side error you should set up
the screw which moves the mirror across,
rather than up and down. It will be found
at one side of the mirror. Don't worry if
this produces a large 'index error' (up
and down error) because the last
adjustment for index error should
remove this.

Index error (see left)

Effect: Images one above the other with the
instrument set at zero.
Cause: Horizon mirror out of adjustment in the
'up and down' plane.
Cure: Adjust the second screw on the horizon
mirror. You may find that this will
reintroduce a little side error; a small
error can be tolerated, but by playing
one adjustment against the other you
may still be able to eliminate both.

If you cannot, then you are stuck with an *index
error*. This, in practice, will not vary with a good
instrument and once quantified should be
allowed for each time you use the sextant.

To quantify your index error, look at a star or the
horizon through the instrument and place the
two images exactly side by side. Then read the
sextant. The reading on the micrometer is the
index error. It should not be more than two or
three minutes and should be labelled *on* or *off*
the arc.

If the sextant is reading + 2 minutes (say),
then your index error is on the arc and should
be subtracted from all your subsequent
readings to render them true. If the instrument
is reading 58 minutes, then your error is two
minutes *off* the arc and you should add two
minutes to your readings. To sum up:

When it's **OFF** (the arc), add it **ON**.
When it's **ON** take it **OFF**.

TRUE ALTITUDE AND SEXTANT ALTITUDE

Having set up your sextant you know that it is
giving the correct altitude for the body - given
the possible regular correction for index error.
Unless you bounce it, it should remain true for
years without further attention. Just check it over
once in a while.

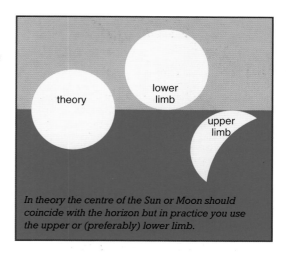

*In theory the centre of the Sun or Moon should
coincide with the horizon but in practice you use
the upper or (preferably) lower limb.*

In order to reduce the altitude you measure
with your sextant to the true altitude of the body
(that is the angle it is making with the *celestial
horizon*) you need to make a few corrections - on
paper this time.

Dip

Just to recap, this is the correction to be applied
because your height of eye enables you to see
beyond the theoretical terrestrial horizon.

In the front of *The Nautical Almanac*, and on
the handout bookmark in every copy, is a group
of tables for correcting your sextant altitude.
You will see the corrections for dip at the
right-hand side of the table on page 35. If you
estimate your height of eye to be, for example,
10 feet or three metres, then the correction for
dip will be minus 3.1 minutes.
Note: *Dip is always subtractive.*

Waves and dip

It is normal on the ocean to have a sea running.
In the northeast trades in mid-Atlantic there will
probably be a ground swell eight to ten feet in
height. In the North Atlantic after heavy weather
there could easily be a swell running to 20 feet
or more. If this is the case you'll have to estimate
the wave height, divide it by two and add the
result to your height of eye; you'll only see the
horizon from the top of a wave, so that is where
you'll be when you take your sight.

Refraction

Because the light from a heavenly body is bent
by the Earth's atmosphere, a correction is
necessary for refraction. Fortunately this is
included, along with parallax and semidiameter
(see next page) where there is any, in the
altitude correction tables.

Semidiameter

If you are observing the Sun or the Moon, you cannot guess accurately where the centre of the body is, and so you place the upper or lower limb (see illustration page 17) on the horizon. The altitude correction tables include the corrections required to convert one limb or the other to the real altitude of the Sun and, as you will see, the Moon makes its own arrangements. When entering the tables for the Sun, notice the two columns: one for northern summer and one for winter. The lower limb is given in bold type because, for some reason, it is much easier to shoot than the upper limb and so is preferred by everyone.

Parallax

The Moon is a law to itself here and will be discussed in due course. The Sun's parallax is covered by the altitude correction tables and needs to be considered no further.

Don't forget, though, that the two closest planets, Venus and Mars, sometimes produce a touch of parallax themselves. The central table shown on page 35 is the total correction (excluding dip and index error, of course) for the stars and planets, but in its right-hand column is a small additional correction to be made in certain months for the parallax of our nearest neighbours.

Notice that the point of entry into the altitude correction tables is *apparent altitude*. This is your sextant altitude corrected for index error (if any) and dip.

Low altitude sights

When heavenly bodies are observed at altitudes below 10°, the refraction produced by the Earth's atmosphere begins to increase rapidly. In practice, this can produce some unreliable results and you should generally avoid taking such a sight.

Occasionally, however, you'll have no option as it may be all that is on offer. If this is the case, you'll find a special set of correction tables to deal with low altitudes near the front of *The Nautical Almanac*. A further table follows to deal with the effects of unusual atmospheric pressure and temperature. These are negligible in practice at normal altitudes, but if you are shooting something very low down, they begin to bite, so take care.

It all adds up to an unpromising picture. Try to keep your altitudes up above the 10° mark and these difficulties will never arise. Here is an example of a sextant altitude correction for a typical Sun sight (lower limb).

Sextant altitude (Hs)	56° 17′	.5
Index error (IE)	— 2′	.1
Dip (height of eye 12′)	— 3′	.4
Apparent altitude (App alt)	56° 12′	.0
Altitude correction (April-Sept)	+ 15′	.3
True altitude (Ho)	56° 27′	.3

Now an example on the same sextant for a star:

Hs	24° 15′	.8
IE	— 2′	.1
Dip (HE 8′)	— 2′	.7
App alt	24° 11′	.0
Correction	— 2′	.1
Ho	24° 8′	.9

When you pick up the sextant, grasp it by the frame, and not by the index bar, scale or telescope.

USING A SEXTANT

Assuming that your sextant is adjusted correctly, and any index error quantified, this is how you use it to measure the altitude of the Sun.

1 Open the box (right way up).
2 Grasp the instrument, by the frame as far as possible, in your left hand and lift it out of the box. Do *not* lift it by the index bar or by the scale.
3 Take the handle in your right hand and sit yourself comfortably and firmly in a suitable position to take your sight. On a large, stable boat like my pilot cutter you can stand on the deck in clement weather, but sitting is usually preferable. You'll need both hands for the sextant - neither is available for either the ship or yourself, so choose a secure site for your posterior.
4 Set the instrument to 'zero' and look towards the horizon to check the *index error*

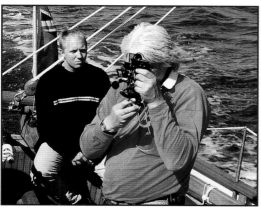

Plant yourself firmly to take a sight.

(see page 17).

5 With the instrument still at zero, drop a shade or two over the index mirror and aim the telescope at the Sun. It may be advisable to put the lightest shade over the horizon mirror as well before you do this, otherwise you could end up with a sore eye.

6 When you have the sun clearly in focus, open the clamp on the index bar with your left hand and, as you sweep the instrument down towards the horizon with your right hand, 'follow' the image of the Sun with your left until it is sitting somewhere near the horizon. This is tricky at first, but it comes with practice.

On all but the brightest days you'll need to remove the shade from the horizon mirror before you use the micrometer to work the Sun's image firmly onto the line of the horizon.

7 It's important that the sextant is exactly

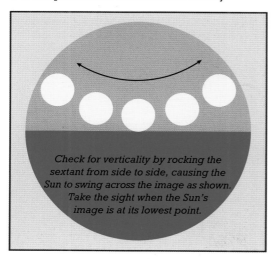

Check for verticality by rocking the sextant from side to side, causing the Sun to swing across the image as shown. Take the sight when the Sun's image is at its lowest point.

vertical when measuring an altitude, so once the sun is approximately in place, you should twist your right wrist from side to side to rock the sextant; as you do this the image of the Sun will appear to 'pendulum' across the horizon. When it is at its lowest point, the sextant is vertical: this is the moment to set the micrometer and read off the altitude.

8 If you catch the Sun at ten o'clock on a midsummer morning its rate of climb will surprise you, but around noon it won't be moving very fast at all, so be ready for both states.

Care of the sextant

Handled carefully, a good sextant requires only minimal day-to-day maintenance. Its moving parts are surprisingly robust, and an occasional drop of light machine oil are all they need. The mirrors are vulnerable to seawater so a rinse-off in fresh water is important if the instrument stops a wave. Try to resist the temptation to polish your sextant at regular intervals, especially if it is a fine brass one. The trouble is that although this makes it look great, it also slowly and steadily wears away the gradations on the scale. By all means shine up the brass telescope if you have one.

Starting out

Use of the sextant is the essence of celestial navigation. If you are ever to be more than marginally competent you will need to be a dab hand with the tools. Sling the sextant in the car, go down to the nearest south-facing beach, and practise, practise, practise. Ignore the wise-guy taunts of the bathers, because you will have the last laugh.

By the time the Sun has set you'll be quite proficient, so treat yourself to a beer and wait for twilight, then see if you can 'pull down' a few stars before night swallows the horizon. Don't worry about which ones they are, just work at the technique.

Only you can teach yourself how to do this, but pretty soon you'll find that you no longer have to start with the sextant at zero. You'll be able to make a guess and look through it in the general direction of the body, then when you have found what you are searching for you can adjust its image down (or up) to the horizon.

The really good news is that if you can do this on the beach or hill, or even from your apartment window using a roof-top as a horizon, you'll be able to do it at sea. For some reason the movement of a boat bothers a sextant far less than it bothers a handbearing compass.

3 The noon sight for latitude

Local noon occurs at the moment when the Sun, on its journey from east to west, crosses the observer's meridian.

At any one time, you are on a particular terrestrial meridian of longitude. When the Sun bears exactly due south or due north of you, or once in a lifetime is right over your head (at your zenith), its celestial meridian (its GHA) will correspond to your longitude.

As we are about to see, if you can observe the altitude of any celestial body when it is exactly on your meridian, a very simple calculation will give you your latitude. Since finding your latitude is half the battle, and since the Sun is very much in evidence at noon, the noon sight has always been the cornerstone of the navigator's day.

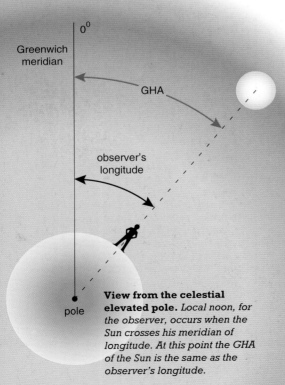

View from the celestial elevated pole. *Local noon, for the observer, occurs when the Sun crosses his meridian of longitude. At this point the GHA of the Sun is the same as the observer's longitude.*

FINDING THE TIME OF LOCAL NOON

Obviously the 'Greenwich' time of noon is going to vary from location to location as the Sun 'goes round the Earth'. When you are sitting on deck with your sextant you can tell when the Sun has reached its noon altitude because it doesn't get any higher.

Nevertheless you don't want to be hanging around all day waiting for it, so you need to be able to work out the approximate time of local noon.

Since the Sun completes its (apparent) journey once every 24 hours, and during that time traverses 360°, it follows that in one hour it will move through 15°, or one degree every four minutes.

The Sun is proceeding west from Greenwich, so if you are in west longitude, your local noon will be *later* than Greenwich, and if you are in east longitude, it will be *earlier*.

To determine how much earlier or later, simply multiply the number of degrees you are east or west of Greenwich by four: this gives you the number of minutes by which your local noon will differ from the time of noon at Greenwich. (There is an arc-to-time conversion table in the almanac that does this for you, if you prefer.)

Have a look at the daily page of the almanac illustrated on page 31, and at the bottom right-hand corner you will see a box labelled SUN and MOON. The column headed 'MER PASS' gives the time that the Sun will cross the Greenwich meridian on that day.

However unsure of your position you may be, you can always take a stab at a DR (dead reckoning) longitude for the time of local noon. Go for a whole degree and make sure you err on the 'early' side. You don't want to miss it.

Example 1

What time is local noon in DR longitude 4°W on May 2nd 1986?

Mer pass at Greenwich	11h 57m
4W W = +	16m
Local noon	12h 13m GMT

Example 2

What time is local noon in DR longitude 73°E on
October 26th 1986?

Mer pass at Greenwich	11h 44m
73E E = —	4h 52m
Local noon	06h 52m GMT

If you happen to be sailing around within a few
degrees of the Date Line on the opposite side of
the globe from the Greenwich Meridian, a query
may arise as to which day it is. If this is so, refer
to Chapter 4, pages 25-6. If not, just remember that
you have calculated the *Greenwich Time* of noon
for your approximate longitude, and read on.

TAKING THE SIGHT

Once you know the approximate time of local
noon, all that remains is to get up on deck
10 minutes or so early and start shooting the
Sun's altitude.

You'll find it is still rising when you begin, but
as it approaches its highest point you will be
'racking it down' slower and slower, until it
stands still for a moment or two. That is the noon
altitude. Whatever you do, don't start to rack the
Sun up again as it begins to fall. Just wait until
the lower limb bites positively into the horizon

without altering the sextant again and you know
you have it. Noon is past and gone for another
day. Note the log; go below, read your sextant,
put it away and then work out your latitude.

THE THEORY

The illustration opposite demonstrates the noon
sight set-up when viewed from the celestial
elevated pole.

The illustration below shows it as seen from
the celestial equator. Note how the celestial
horizon makes a right-angle with the line
dropped from the observer's zenith, through his
geographic position to the centre of the Earth.
Zenith Distance (ZD) is the only new concept to
grab hold of. It is, quite simply, the angular
distance (measured in degrees) between the
observer's zenith and the position of the Sun
on the celestial sphere.

Since the line from the observer's zenith
meets the celestial horizon at 90°, the zenith
distance must equal 90° minus the Sun's altitude:

ZD = 90° — ALTITUDE

You can see from the illustration below that
latitude is the same angle on the terrestrial
sphere as ZD + declination is on the celestial.
Declination can be found in the almanac, and
you can easily work out ZD.

Add them together, and that's your latitude -
given that your latitude is greater than the Sun's
declination, and of the same 'name' (i.e. north or

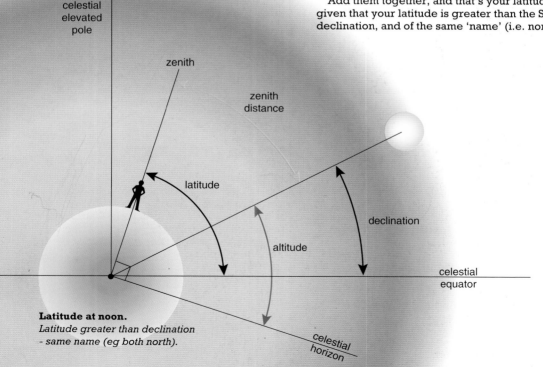

Latitude at noon.
*Latitude greater than declination
- same name (eg both north).*

Latitude and declination with different names.

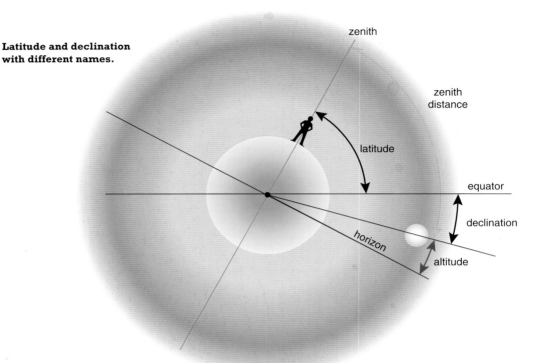

south), as it is in this case:

LAT = ZD + DEC

However, quite frequently, depending upon the season and where you are, latitude and declination will have different names and relative values. There are two other cases which may arise. In the diagram above, the latitude is the opposite 'name' to the declination and you can see that LAT = ZD — DEC.
The diagram opposite illustrates a situation that you meet in the tropics, where your latitude may be the same name as the declination, but could well be a lower value (e.g. latitude 12°N, Sun's declination 22°N). Here, LAT = DEC —ZD.

Spelled out in rote rule form, latitudes can be expressed as follows:

Latitude GREATER than declination. Same name:
LAT = ZD + DEC

Latitude OPPOSITE name to declination:
LAT = ZD — DEC

Latitude LESS than declination. Same name:
LAT = DEC — ZD

In practice, unless your voyage passes 'under'

the Sun or takes place during an equinox when the Sun's declination changes name, you'll have to make this decision only once per trip. The answer is the same every day.

So, to work a noon sight, what do you need?

• A *corrected* sextant altitude (Ho).
• The zenith distance (ZD = 90° — Ho).
• The declination of the Sun at the time of your sight (*not* at Greenwich noon, please!)
Insert ZD and DEC into one of the three formulae and...

YOU HAVE A LATITUDE

Example
2nd May 1986. Your DR is 50° 25′N 7°W. Local noon is therefore 1225 GMT. This enables you to obtain the declination of the Sun (DEC) from the almanac. Using the sextant, you find that the Sun's *corrected* altitude (Ho) at noon is 54° 47′.4. What is your latitude?

LAT = ZD + DEC

Dec 12h	N 15° 22′ .4
+ 25m ('d' = + 0.7)	0′ .3
Dec 1225	N 15° 22′ .7

Latitude less than declination, same name.

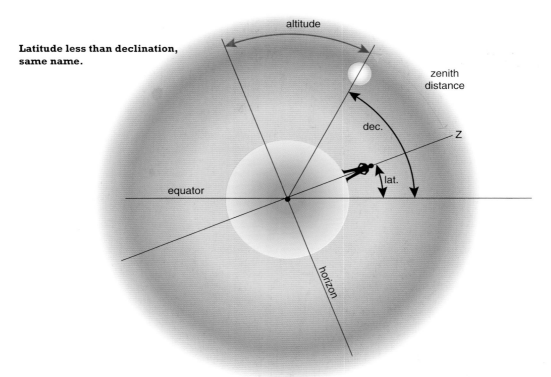

90	89° 60′
— Ho	54° 47′ .4
= ZD	35° 12′ .6
+ Dec	N 15° 22′ .7
Lat	N 50° 35′ .3

(* To make the subtraction easier I always express 90° as 89° 60'. It gives you less figures to carry.)

OTHER BODIES

The theory of working out a latitude from a body on your meridian holds good for everything in the sky, not just the Sun. The Sun is the most popular, though, because it is on the meridian at noon and can be employed in conjunction with a forenoon sight (see Chapter 6) to produce a fix, but don't discount the possibility of using a suitable star at twilight, a planet, or the Moon. A latitude is a very useful thing to have.

'MAXIMUM' ALTITUDES

In theory, the system described above for determining latitude works perfectly only from a stationary vessel, or one which is travelling exactly east or west. The reason is that if you are in the northern hemisphere and sailing southwards towards the Sun (your latitude being greater than its declination), your changing latitude will cause the Sun to continue to 'rise' while it is actually past your meridian. Similarly if you were moving in a northerly direction, the Sun's altitude would begin to decrease before it reached your meridian.

For a fast-moving ship doing 20 knots or so due north or south, this can produce errors of up to five minutes of arc. In a sailing yacht working manfully to keep up her five knots it is rarely a factor to consider. However, if you have a big north/south component in your course, bear in mind that your latitude from a meridian sight may not be quite as accurate as you would hope.

Allowing for the maximum altitude effect

Since the Sun is crossing the meridians at the rate of one every four minutes you should, unless your DR is wildly astray, be able to work out to the nearest minute or so the time that the Sun will pass the meridian of your noon DR longitude.

Take the Sun's altitude at about this time instead of waiting for it to reach its highest point, and that will be as near to the meridian altitude as you are going to get. Remember that, this close to noon, if the altitude is changing at all, it will be changing very slowly.

4 Time

In Chapter 3, while considering the Greenwich time of local noon for our longitude, we looked at the basic relationship of arc and time, and found it to be:

ONE DAY = 360°
ONE HOUR = 360° ÷ 24 = 15°
FOUR MINUTES = 1°

However, whereas a degree can be defined as 1/360 of a circle, the definition of a day is not quite so clear-cut. This is because, amongst other things, the Earth is travelling in its orbit round the Sun at the same time as it revolves, and orbits are sometimes a little less regular than the mathematicians would desire.

A suitable definition of a day might be the time taken for the Sun to proceed from our nadir (midnight) through sunrise, across our meridian, down through sunset and back to our nadir once more. Unfortunately, when measured in hours this does not take exactly the same amount of time on every occasion, so to make life tolerable for us all, we must compute an average time for it.

Since the celestial co-ordinates for every day are tabulated in one nautical almanac it was decided long ago to refer them all to the average (or *mean*) time as measured at the Greenwich Observatory, England, giving us our old friend Greenwich Mean Time (GMT).

THE 'MEAN SUN' AND THE 'APPARENT SUN'

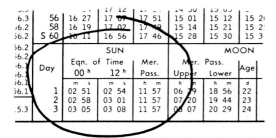

		SUN			MOON		
Day	Eqn. of Time		Mer. Pass.	Mer. Pass.		Age
	00 h	12 h	Pass.	Upper	Lower	
	m s	m s	h m	h m	h m	d
1	02 51	02 54	11 57	06 29	18 56	22
2	02 58	03 01	11 57	07 20	19 44	23
3	03 05	03 08	11 57	08 07	20 29	24

The actual time of the Sun's meridian passage, and the difference between this and noon GMT, is given in the daily pages of the almanac.

The *mean* Sun is the imaginary body moving with perfect regularity from which GMT is taken. It represents an average of the motions of the *true* or *apparent* Sun (both words have the same meaning in this instance). The mean Sun and the apparent Sun are frequently well adrift from one another.

The difference between the two is called the equation of time and is to be found in the same box as the time of the Sun's meridian passage in the daily pages of the almanac. If, for example, the Sun were 1° 30' East of Greenwich at noon GMT, this equation of time would be six minutes.

Although this figure is seldom used in practice, the fact that there is a difference between the mean and apparent Sun makes it important to check the actual time of the Sun's meridian passage (i.e. apparent noon) each day before deciding when to take your noon sight.

ZONE TIME

Navigators and astronomers may be content to live their lives by GMT, but the general public spoil all that by insisting on lunching at 1300 hours, no matter where they are, and expecting the Sun to rise at 0600. They set their clocks by the movement of the Sun and, in consequence, 'working time' alters from place to place around the globe.

In fact, the time of sunrise, say, varies with every step you take east or west, but if each town and village worked to its own time the result would be chaos. In order to simplify this business the world is divided into 24 *time zones*. Not surprisingly, each time zone is 15° of longitude across.

Each meridian divisible by 15 is a *zone meridian* and its time zone spreads out 7½° to either side of it.

NAMING THE ZONES: '+' or '—'

Since the Sun rises in the east and proceeds to the westward across the sky it follows that it will rise later in 90°W than it does at Greenwich. Actually it will rise 90÷15, or six hours later. So when the Sun is rising at 0600 at Greenwich, it is midnight (0000 hours) in Chicago at 90°W.

0600 GMT

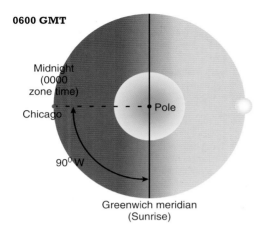

Greenwich meridian
(Sunrise)

1200 GMT

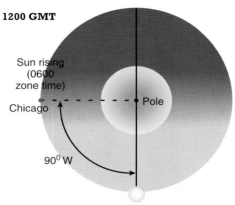

Noon at Greenwich
(Sun on meridian)

Six hours later, when the Sun does rise in Chicago, the time there will be, conveniently, 0600 hours.
By then it will be 1200 (noon) at Greenwich and nearly time for lunch.

At any given instant, if you have your watch set to Chicago time and you want to convert it to Greenwich, you'll have to *add* six hours. Chicago is therefore said to be in 'Zone + 6'. In the same way, all the western time zones, right round to the International Date Line, are named 'plus'.

All the eastern time zones are named 'minus'. The Sun rises in, say, Moscow before it does at Greenwich, so zone time at Moscow will be later than Greenwich and you'll have to subtract the relevant number of hours to reduce Moscow time to Greenwich time.

The divisions between time zones, for reasons of national convenience, do not always fall exactly halfway between the zone meridians concerned. France, for example, in order to fit in with the rest of continental Europe, has placed itself in 'Zone - 1', although most of its land mass falls plumb into the Greenwich time zone.

This sort of thing won't affect your ship's working clock in mid-ocean, but it is as well to be aware of it. Tide tables, for example, are usually issued in the official zone time of the country concerned, regardless of its longitude.

A few examples
Since all tabulated celestial data refer to GMT, you will constantly be converting from your ship's zone time to Greenwich time and vice versa. Once again, practice makes it easy, but in the meantime here are some examples to clarify the matter:

Q What time zone are you in if your longitude is 170°W?
A Zone + 11.
Q What will your ship's clock say at 1000 GMT in 10°E longitude?
A 10°E is Zone - 1. This means that you must subtract one hour from your zone time to get down to Greenwich, so your zone time must be 1100.
Q Which meridian will you have crossed on a westbound passage of the north Atlantic when the ship's clock goes back from GMT - 3 to GMT - 4? (Remember that in west longitude, you are in Zone + 3 and moving to Zone + 4 as you move away from Greenwich. At any time you must add time to your zone time to get up to Greenwich, so your ship's clock will show an earlier time than Greenwich. Remember that the man in Chicago was getting up when the Greenwich observer sat down to his lunch.)
A The zone meridian for Zone + 3 is 3 x 15° = 45°W.
The zone meridian for Zone + 4 is 4 x 15° = 60°W.
Halfway between the two you change zones, so the boundary between Zone + 3 and Zone + 4 falls at 52$\frac{1}{2}$°W. (See diagram page 26.)

Change of date and the International Date Line
Watch out for this one. If it arises, tackle it logically and it will present no problem. Let us assume you are in Zone + 8. It is 1830 zone time (ZT) on March 25th. What is GMT? If you are in Zone + 8, you will add eight hours to 1830 ZT and come up with 2630 GMT on March 25th. Obviously this means 0230 GMT on March 26th. That's better.

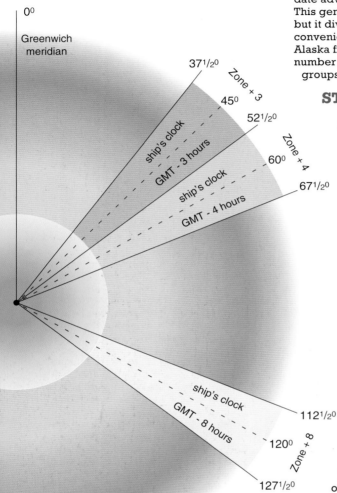

0°

Greenwich
meridian

37 1/2°

Zone + 3

45°

52 1/2°

ship's clock

GMT - 3 hours

Zone + 4

60°

ship's clock

67 1/2°

GMT - 4 hours

ship's clock

GMT - 8 hours

112 1/2°

120°

Zone + 8

127 1/2°

date advances for ease of administration. This generally follows the 180th meridian, but it diverts here and there for the sake of convenience. The zig-zag which separates Alaska from Siberia is a case in point, as are a number of kinks which keep Pacific island groups together.

STANDARD TIME

In order to make best use of the local electricity supplies by extending daylight into the evenings, many countries choose to add one hour (or even two hours) to their zone time during the summer.

These arrangements are purely domestic and have no relevance to the astro-navigator, but if you are setting sail on a voyage from a country operating such an arrangement, don't forget to set your ship's clock to something more sensible as soon as you leave, or you may have a debacle.

It's also important to be aware of standard time when you arrive or you may be caught out by that greatest of disasters: to step ashore after crossing an ocean only to discover that the pubs have just shut.

THE NAVIGATION CLOCK

Just in case you have a mental block on questions of time when you are at sea, all problems can be solved by referring to your navigation clock, which you should keep set on GMT. Even if you actually time your sights with your quartz wristwatch, as I do, you should always have a back-up clock somewhere on board. Personally I keep my wristwatch on zone time, which on my boat is usually ship's time, but if my mind blows a fuse while thrashing to windward when I am dog tired, I can always refer to the navigation clock to check up on GMT.

While this arrangement will stand you in good stead for navigational purposes, it does not do to forget the International Date Line which runs north-south from pole to pole and where the

5 Position lines and plotting

As with coastal navigation, a position obtained using astro-navigation techniques is plotted on a chart using position lines (PLs), but instead of being straight, these are (theoretically) circular. Most of the position lines used in coastal navigation are straight lines, but there are one or two sources of PL, generally thought of as methods of determining 'distance off', which are in fact circular lines of position.

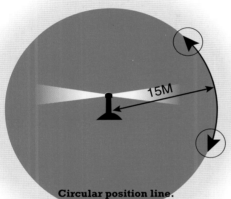

Circular position line.
If you know your distance from a lighthouse but you have no compass, you know that you are somewhere on a circular position line

Consider, for example, the 'rising' or 'dipping' lighthouse. The tables tell us that with a height of eye of eight feet we will see such and such a light 'rise' at a distance of 15 miles. When it pops up we dutifully take a magnetic bearing and mark off our position 15 miles out from the lighthouse. If we didn't have any means of determining the bearing of the light, however, we would be left with just the knowledge that we were 15 miles from it. We could scribe a circle 15 miles in radius

around it and know that we would be somewhere on that circle.

In astro-navigation, all the PLs are actually parts of a circle scribed around the geographic position (on the terrestrial sphere) of the body observed, but the circles are so huge that a short section of the circle looks like a straight line.

AZIMUTH

For such a huge circle to be usable you need to know which section of it to draw on your chart. To determine this you employ a line which gives the bearing of the body from your rough position (in degrees True) and then construct your PL at right angles to it. This 'bearing line' is called an azimuth (Zn) and is defined as 'the

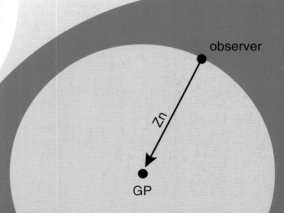

If you know the altitude of a star, you can locate yourself on a circle of position because the altitude of the star will be the same from any point on the circle. The azimuth (Zn) is a bearing to the geographic posiiton (GP) that tells you which part of the circle to use.

circle of position

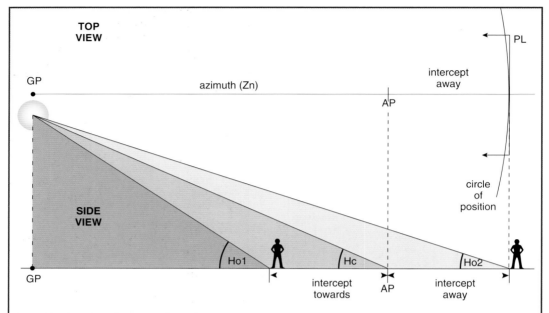

The side view shows how the difference between observed altitude (Ho) and calculated altitude (Hc) is used to find the direction of the intercept from the assumed position (AP). If Ho is less than Hc, for example, the intercept is away from the celestial body, as shown in the top view. Notice that the PL is actually at a tangent to the circle of position.

horizontal direction of a celestial point from a terrestrial point'. (Incidentally, the word is pronounced 'azzmuth'.)

To work up a PL, first calculate what the altitude and azimuth of the body would be at the time of your sight from a convenient assumed position (AP). This should be as close as possible to where you think you are (your DR position), but is rarely the same. This is because the AP is selected to fit in with the information in the almanac and sight reduction tables which is presented in convenient 'steps' of whole degrees. The technique of calculating the altitude and azimuth of the body from the AP is described in Chapter 6.

Because the distances from both your DR and AP to the geographic position of the body are so enormous, the azimuth to either position can be considered to be the same. The altitude that you have observed using your sextant, however, is usually different from the one you have calculated from your assumed position. This difference, which is measured in minutes of arc, is called the *intercept* and can be expressed on the chart as minutes of latitude, or nautical miles. In effect, your AP is functioning as a datum, and the intercept gives you the distance from this

datum to your position line.

In the diagram above you can see what all this actually means. You will notice that if the observed altitude from your actual position (Ho) is greater than the calculated altitude at the

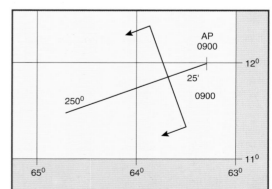

A position line (PL) plotted on a chart. The azimuth has been drawn in at 250° from the AP, and the PL drawn across it at right angles 25' from the AP towards the body.

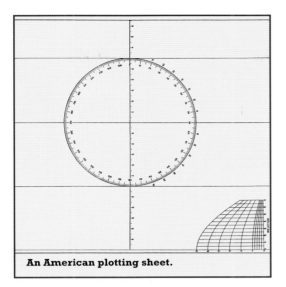

An American plotting sheet.

1 Mark the assumed position (AP).
2 Draw the azimuth (Zn) passing through it.
3 Decide whether the intercept is towards or away from the body. In this case it is towards. The Zn is 250° which means that the body bears 250° from the AP, so you measure off the intercept in that direction.
4 Construct your PL, which will pass through the intercept at right angles to the azimuth. The PL is marked as a straight line with arrowheads at each end pointing towards the body.

Note: The point at which the PL crosses the azimuth is NOT A FIX. It is merely a reference point from which to construct your PL, which has much the same function as a bearing line from an observed object such as a buoy. To achieve a fix you need at least one more PL. More about this later.

Plotting charts

If you are sailing in coastal waters you can usually plot your sights directly onto your working chart. In mid-ocean, however, the scale of the chart makes accurate plotting impossible. Instead, use a plotting chart.

These can be made up yourself, but they are so cheap to buy that I always kit up with a sheaf before I set sail. They are recyclable, so don't worry about having enough to last the voyage. Plotting charts come in various forms with a variety of scales. I prefer those issued by the United States Defense Mapping Agency. The scale is realistic and with careful use of a sharp pencil a whole day's run can be fitted onto one chart.

The illustration shows a blank of this form. To use it designate one of the transverse lines as your assumed latitude and then take measurements for your assumed longitude from the scale at the bottom right-hand corner. All further measurements of intercept, etc., are marked off utilising the latitude scale printed down the middle of the sheet.

The compass rose is there purely for the convenience of those plotting with parallel rulers. Personally I always use a Douglas (square) Protractor for plotting astro PLs. Once you have fixed your position on the plotting chart, you can express it in terms of latitude and longitude, log it and transfer it to your ocean chart.

assumed position (Hc), then the PL will be nearer to the geographic position (GP) of the body. Conversely, if the Ho is less than the Hc, the PL will be further away.

Because the assumed position is effectively on the same azimuth as your actual position you never need to know what the GP of the body really is. You simply draw a short section of the azimuth through the assumed position on your chart. Then, if the Ho is *greater* than the Hc, you mark off your intercept so many miles *in the direction* of the body. If the Ho is less than the Hc, mark it off *away* from it. Then you draw your PL through your intercept, at right angles to the azimuth.

The rule to remember for which way to mark off your intercept is this:

Calculated **(Tabulated)** altitude less **(Tinier)** than observed altitude: intercept **Towards** the body.
Tabulated; Tinier; Towards - TTT

Clearly, if the Ho is less than the Hc the converse will apply. Intercepts are always labelled 'towards' or 'away'.

PRACTICAL PLOTTING

Illustrated above is a section of a chart. In order to plot a sight all you have to do is:

1986 MAY 1, 2, 3 (THURS., FRI., SAT.)

G.M.T. (UT)	ARIES G.H.A.	VENUS −3.3 G.H.A.	Dec.	MARS −0.5 G.H.A.	Dec.	JUPITER −1.7 G.H.A.	Dec.	SATURN +0.3 G.H.A.	Dec.	STARS Name	S.H.A.	Dec.
1 00	218 37.7	155 34.7	N21 49.4	292 06.7	S23 43.5	231 43.9	S 6 40.4	331 44.2	S19 41.3	Acamar	315 34.3	S40 21.6
01	233 40.2	170 34.0	50.1	307 08.1	43.5	246 46.0	40.3	346 46.8	41.3	Achernar	335 42.4	S57 18.3
02	248 42.6	185 33.3	50.7	322 09.6	43.5	261 48.0	40.1	1 49.5	41.3	Acrux	173 32.3	S63 01.6
03	263 45.1	200 32.5	·· 51.4	337 11.0	·· 43.5	276 50.0	·· 39.9	16 52.1	·· 41.3	Adhara	255 29.0	S28 57.3
04	278 47.5	215 31.8	52.0	352 12.5	43.5	291 52.0	39.8	31 54.7	41.2	Aldebaran	291 13.5	N16 29.0
05	293 50.0	230 31.0	52.7	7 14.0	43.5	306 54.1	39.6	46 57.3	41.2			
06	308 52.5	245 30.3	N21 53.3	22 15.4	S23 43.5	321 56.1	S 6 39.4	62 00.0	S19 41.2	Alioth	166 38.0	N56 02.1
07	323 54.9	260 29.6	54.0	37 16.9	43.5	336 58.1	39.2	77 02.6	41.2	Alkaid	153 14.5	N49 22.9
T 08	338 57.4	275 28.8	54.6	52 18.3	43.5	352 00.2	39.1	92 05.2	41.1	Al Na'ir	28 09.6	S47 01.6
H 09	353 59.9	290 28.1	·· 55.3	67 19.8	·· 43.5	7 02.2	·· 38.9	107 07.8	·· 41.1	Alnilam	276 07.6	S 1 12.6
U 10	9 02.3	305 27.3	55.9	82 21.3	43.5	22 04.2	38.7	122 10.4	41.1	Alphard	218 16.4	S 8 36.0
R 11	24 04.8	320 26.6	56.6	97 22.7	43.5	37 06.3	38.6	137 13.1	41.1			
S 12	39 07.3	335 25.9	N21 57.2	112 24.2	S23 43.6	52 08.3	S 6 38.4	152 15.7	S19 41.0	Alphecca	126 28.1	N26 45.4
D 13	54 09.7	350 25.1	57.9	127 25.7	43.6	67 10.4	38.2	167 18.3	41.0	Alpheratz	358 05.3	N29 00.7
A 14	69 12.2	5 24.4	58.5	142 27.1	43.6	82 12.4	38.0	182 20.9	41.0	Altair	62 28.3	N 8 49.6
Y 15	84 14.7	20 23.6	·· 59.1	157 28.6	·· 43.6	97 14.4	·· 37.9	197 23.6	·· 41.0	Ankaa	353 36.2	S42 22.8
16	99 17.1	35 22.9	21 59.8	172 30.1	43.6	112 16.5	37.7	212 26.2	40.9	Antares	112 51.4	S26 24.3
17	114 19.6	50 22.1	22 00.4	187 31.5	43.6	127 18.5	37.5	227 28.8	40.9			
18	129 22.0	65 21.4	N22 01.1	202 33.0	S23 43.6	142 20.5	S 6 37.4	242 31.4	S19 40.9	Arcturus	146 14.2	N19 15.1
19	144 24.5	80 20.7	01.7	217 34.5	43.6	157 22.6	37.2	257 34.1	40.8	Atria	108 11.5	S69 00.2
20	159 27.0	95 19.9	02.3	232 35.9	43.6	172 24.6	37.0	272 36.7	40.8	Avior	234 26.8	S59 28.1
21	174 29.4	110 19.2	·· 03.0	247 37.4	·· 43.6	187 26.6	·· 36.9	287 39.3	·· 40.8	Bellatrix	278 54.5	N 6 20.3
22	189 31.9	125 18.4	03.6	262 38.9	43.6	202 28.7	36.7	302 41.9	40.8	Betelgeuse	271 23.9	N 7 24.4
23	204 34.4	140 17.7	04.2	277 40.3	43.6	217 30.7	36.5	317 44.6	40.7			
2 00	219 36.8	155 16.9	N22 04.9	292 41.8	S23 43.6	232 32.7	S 6 36.3	332 47.2	S19 40.7	Canopus	264 05.7	S52 41.4
01	234 39.3	170 16.2	05.5	307 43.3	43.6	247 34.8	36.2	347 49.8	40.7	Capella	281 05.5	N45 59.3
02	249 41.8	185 15.4	06.1	322 44.8	43.6	262 36.8	36.0	2 52.5	40.7	Deneb	49 45.7	N45 13.4
03	264 44.2	200 14.7	·· 06.8	337 46.2	·· 43.6	277 38.8	·· 35.8	17 55.1	·· 40.6	Denebola	182 54.4	N14 38.9
04	279 46.7	215 13.9	07.4	352 47.7	43.6	292 40.9	35.7	32 57.7	40.6	Diphda	349 16.8	S18 03.8
05	294 49.2	230 13.2	08.0	7 49.2	43.6	307 42.9	35.5	48 00.3	40.6			
06	309 51.6	245 12.4	N22 08.6	22 50.6	S23 43.6	322 45.0	S 6 35.3	63 03.0	S19 40.6	Dubhe	194 16.2	N61 49.8
07	324 54.1	260 11.7	09.3	37 52.1	43.6	337 47.0	35.2	78 05.6	40.5	Elnath	278 39.1	N28 35.9
08	339 56.5	275 10.9	09.9	52 53.6	43.6	352 49.0	35.0	93 08.2	40.5	Eltanin	90 55.4	N51 29.0
F 09	354 59.0	290 10.2	·· 10.5	67 55.1	·· 43.6	7 51.1	·· 34.8	108 10.8	·· 40.5	Enif	34 07.5	N 9 48.4
R 10	10 01.5	305 09.4	11.1	82 56.6	43.7	22 53.1	34.6	123 13.5	40.5	Fomalhaut	15 46.8	S29 41.7
I 11	25 03.9	320 08.7	11.8	97 58.0	43.7	37 55.1	34.5	138 16.1	40.4			
D 12	40 06.4	335 07.9	N22 12.4	112 59.5	S23 43.7	52 57.2	S 6 34.3	153 18.7	S19 40.4	Gacrux	172 23.9	S57 02.4
A 13	55 08.9	350 07.2	13.0	128 01.0	43.7	67 59.2	34.1	168 21.3	40.4	Gienah	176 13.4	S17 28.1
Y 14	70 11.3	5 06.4	13.6	143 02.5	43.7	83 01.3	34.0	183 24.0	40.4	Hadar	149 17.0	S60 18.6
15	85 13.8	20 05.7	·· 14.2	158 04.0	·· 43.7	98 03.3	·· 33.8	198 26.6	·· 40.3	Hamal	328 24.6	N23 23.8
16	100 16.3	35 04.9	14.8	173 05.4	43.7	113 05.3	33.6	213 29.2	40.3	Kaus Aust.	84 11.0	S34 23.6
17	115 18.7	50 04.2	15.5	188 06.9	43.7	128 07.4	33.5	228 31.9	40.3			
18	130 21.2	65 03.4	N22 16.1	203 08.4	S23 43.7	143 09.4	S 6 33.3	243 34.5	S19 40.2	Kochab	137 17.4	N74 12.6
19	145 23.6	80 02.7	16.7	218 09.9	43.7	158 11.5	33.1	258 37.1	40.2	Markab	13 59.2	N15 07.6
20	160 26.1	95 01.9	17.3	233 11.4	43.7	173 13.5	33.0	273 39.7	40.2	Menkar	314 37.0	N 4 02.2
21	175 28.6	110 01.2	·· 17.9	248 12.9	·· 43.7	188 15.5	·· 32.8	288 42.4	·· 40.2	Menkent	148 31.8	S36 18.3
22	190 31.0	125 00.4	18.6	263 14.4	43.7	203 17.6	32.6	303 45.0	40.1	Miaplacidus	221 44.4	S69 39.9
23	205 33.5	139 59.6	19.1	278 15.8	43.7	218 19.6	32.4	318 47.6	40.1			
3 00	220 36.0	154 58.9	N22 19.7	293 17.3	S23 43.7	233 21.7	S 6 32.3	333 50.2	S19 40.1	Mirfak	309 10.7	N49 48.8
01	235 38.4	169 58.1	20.3	308 18.8	43.7	248 23.7	32.1	348 52.9	40.1	Nunki	76 23.7	S26 19.0
02	250 40.9	184 57.4	20.9	323 20.3	43.7	263 25.7	31.9	3 55.5	40.0	Peacock	53 51.4	S56 46.7
03	265 43.4	199 56.6	·· 21.5	338 21.8	·· 43.7	278 27.8	·· 31.8	18 58.1	·· 40.0	Pollux	243 53.1	N28 03.8
04	280 45.8	214 55.9	22.1	353 23.3	43.8	293 29.8	31.6	34 00.8	40.0	Procyon	245 21.5	N 5 15.7
05	295 48.3	229 55.1	22.7	8 24.8	43.8	308 31.9	31.4	49 03.4	40.0			
06	310 50.8	244 54.3	N22 23.3	23 26.3	S23 43.8	323 33.9	S 6 31.3	64 06.0	S19 39.9	Rasalhague	96 25.4	N12 33.9
07	325 53.2	259 53.6	23.9	38 27.8	43.8	338 35.9	31.1	79 08.6	39.9	Regulus	208 05.4	N12 02.1
S 08	340 55.7	274 52.8	24.5	53 29.3	43.8	353 38.0	30.9	94 11.3	39.9	Rigel	281 32.2	S 8 13.0
A 09	355 58.1	289 52.1	·· 25.1	68 30.8	·· 43.8	8 40.0	·· 30.8	109 13.9	·· 39.9	Rigil Kent.	140 19.7	S60 46.8
T 10	11 00.6	304 51.3	25.7	83 32.3	43.8	23 42.1	30.6	124 16.5	39.8	Sabik	102 36.0	S15 42.7
U 11	26 03.1	319 50.5	26.3	98 33.8	43.8	38 44.1	30.4	139 19.2	39.8			
R 12	41 05.5	334 49.8	N22 26.9	113 35.2	S23 43.8	53 46.1	S 6 30.3	154 21.8	S19 39.8	Schedar	350 05.0	N56 27.5
D 13	56 08.0	349 49.0	27.5	128 36.7	43.8	68 48.2	30.1	169 24.4	39.7	Shaula	96 49.7	S37 05.8
A 14	71 10.5	4 48.3	28.1	143 38.2	43.8	83 50.2	29.9	184 27.1	39.7	Sirius	258 52.1	S16 41.9
Y 15	86 12.9	19 47.5	·· 28.7	158 39.7	·· 43.8	98 52.3	·· 29.8	199 29.7	·· 39.7	Spica	158 52.8	S11 05.5
16	101 15.4	34 46.7	29.3	173 41.2	43.8	113 54.3	29.6	214 32.3	39.7	Suhail	223 07.8	S43 22.8
17	116 17.9	49 46.0	29.9	188 42.7	43.8	128 56.4	29.4	229 34.9	39.6			
18	131 20.3	64 45.2	N22 30.5	203 44.2	S23 43.8	143 58.4	S 6 29.3	244 37.6	S19 39.6	Vega	80 52.8	N38 45.8
19	146 22.8	79 44.5	31.0	218 45.7	43.9	159 00.4	29.1	259 40.2	39.6	Zuben'ubi	137 28.1	S15 59.3
20	161 25.3	94 43.7	31.6	233 47.3	43.9	174 02.5	28.9	274 42.8	39.6		S.H.A.	Mer. Pass.
21	176 27.7	109 42.9	·· 32.2	248 48.8	·· 43.9	189 04.5	·· 28.8	289 45.5	·· 39.5			h m
22	191 30.2	124 42.2	32.8	263 50.3	43.9	204 06.6	28.6	304 48.1	39.5	Venus	295 40.1	13 40
23	206 32.6	139 41.4	33.4	278 51.8	43.9	219 08.6	28.4	319 50.7	39.5	Mars	73 05.0	4 29
Mer. Pass.	h m 9 20.0	v −0.8	d 0.6	v 1.5	d 0.0	v 2.0	d 0.2	v 2.6	d 0.0	Jupiter	12 55.9	8 29
										Saturn	113 10.4	1 49

Table 1. Daily Page from The Nautical Almanac..

1986 MAY 1, 2, 3 (THURS., FRI., SAT.)

G.M.T. (UT)	SUN G.H.A.	Dec.	MOON G.H.A.	v	Dec.	d	H.P.
1 00	180 42.7	N14 55.3	266 09.8	08.1	S23 09.8	09.7	58.1
01	195 42.8	56.0	280 36.9	08.1	23 00.1	09.8	58.1
02	210 42.9	56.8	295 04.0	08.3	22 50.3	09.9	58.1
03	225 42.9	.. 57.6	309 31.3	08.4	22 40.4	10.0	58.0
04	240 43.0	58.3	323 58.7	08.6	22 30.4	10.2	58.0
05	255 43.1	59.1	338 26.3	08.7	22 20.2	10.3	58.0
06	270 43.2	N14 59.9	352 54.0	08.7	S22 09.9	10.3	57.9
T 07	285 43.3	15 00.6	7 21.7	09.0	21 59.6	10.5	57.9
H 08	300 43.3	01.4	21 49.7	09.0	21 49.1	10.6	57.9
U 09	315 43.4	.. 02.1	36 17.7	09.2	21 38.5	10.7	57.8
R 10	330 43.5	02.9	50 45.9	09.2	21 27.8	10.8	57.8
S 11	345 43.6	03.6	65 14.1	09.5	21 17.0	10.9	57.8
D 12	0 43.6	N15 04.4	79 42.6	09.5	S21 06.1	11.0	57.7
A 13	15 43.7	05.2	94 11.1	09.6	20 55.1	11.1	57.7
Y 14	30 43.8	05.9	108 39.7	09.8	20 44.0	11.3	57.7
15	45 43.9	.. 06.7	123 08.5	09.9	20 32.7	11.3	57.6
16	60 43.9	07.4	137 37.4	10.0	20 21.4	11.4	57.6
17	75 44.0	08.2	152 06.4	10.1	20 10.0	11.4	57.6
18	90 44.1	N15 08.9	166 35.5	10.2	S19 58.6	11.6	57.6
19	105 44.2	09.7	181 04.7	10.4	19 47.0	11.7	57.5
20	120 44.2	10.4	195 34.1	10.4	19 35.3	11.7	57.5
21	135 44.3	.. 11.2	210 03.5	10.6	19 23.6	11.9	57.5
22	150 44.4	11.9	224 33.1	10.7	19 11.7	11.9	57.4
23	165 44.5	12.7	239 02.8	10.8	18 59.8	12.0	57.4
2 00	180 44.5	N15 13.4	253 32.6	11.0	S18 47.8	12.1	57.4
01	195 44.6	14.2	268 02.6	11.0	18 35.7	12.2	57.3
02	210 44.7	14.9	282 32.6	11.1	18 23.5	12.2	57.3
03	225 44.8	.. 15.7	297 02.7	11.3	18 11.3	12.4	57.3
04	240 44.8	16.4	311 33.0	11.3	17 58.9	12.4	57.2
05	255 44.9	17.2	326 03.3	11.5	17 46.5	12.5	57.2
06	270 45.0	N15 17.9	340 33.8	11.6	S17 34.0	12.5	57.2
F 07	285 45.1	18.7	355 04.4	11.7	17 21.5	12.6	57.1
R 08	300 45.1	19.4	9 35.1	11.7	17 08.9	12.7	57.1
I 09	315 45.2	.. 20.2	24 05.8	11.9	16 56.2	12.8	57.1
D 10	330 45.3	20.9	38 36.7	12.0	16 43.4	12.8	57.1
A 11	345 45.3	21.7	53 07.7	12.1	16 30.6	12.9	57.0
Y 12	0 45.4	N15 22.4	67 38.8	12.2	S16 17.7	13.0	57.0
13	15 45.5	23.2	82 10.0	12.3	16 04.7	13.1	57.0
14	30 45.5	23.9	96 41.3	12.4	15 51.7	13.1	56.9
15	45 45.6	.. 24.7	111 12.7	12.4	15 38.6	13.1	56.9
16	60 45.7	25.4	125 44.1	12.6	15 25.5	13.2	56.9
17	75 45.8	26.2	140 15.7	12.7	15 12.3	13.3	56.9
18	90 45.8	N15 26.9	154 47.4	12.7	S14 59.0	13.3	56.8
19	105 45.9	27.6	169 19.1	12.9	14 45.7	13.3	56.8
20	120 46.0	28.4	183 51.0	12.9	14 32.4	13.5	56.8
21	135 46.0	.. 29.1	198 22.9	13.1	14 18.9	13.6	56.7
22	150 46.1	29.9	212 55.0	13.1	14 05.3	13.6	56.7
23	165 46.2	30.6	227 27.1	13.2	13 51.9	13.5	56.7
3 00	180 46.2	N15 31.4	241 59.3	13.3	S13 38.4	13.7	56.7
01	195 46.3	32.1	256 31.6	13.4	13 24.7	13.6	56.6
02	210 46.4	32.8	271 04.0	13.5	13 11.1	13.7	56.6
03	225 46.4	.. 33.6	285 36.5	13.5	12 57.4	13.8	56.6
04	240 46.5	34.3	300 09.0	13.6	12 43.6	13.8	56.5
05	255 46.6	35.0	314 41.6	13.8	12 29.8	13.8	56.5
06	270 46.6	N15 35.8	329 14.4	13.7	S12 16.0	13.9	56.5
S 07	285 46.7	36.5	343 47.1	13.9	12 02.1	13.9	56.5
A 08	300 46.8	37.3	358 20.0	13.9	11 48.2	14.0	56.4
T 09	315 46.8	.. 38.0	12 52.9	14.1	11 34.2	14.0	56.4
U 10	330 46.9	38.7	27 26.0	14.1	11 20.2	14.0	56.4
R 11	345 47.0	39.5	41 59.1	14.1	11 06.2	14.1	56.4
D 12	0 47.0	N15 40.2	56 32.2	14.3	S10 52.1	14.1	56.3
A 13	15 47.1	40.9	71 05.5	14.3	10 38.0	14.2	56.3
Y 14	30 47.2	41.7	85 38.8	14.3	10 23.8	14.2	56.3
15	45 47.2	.. 42.4	100 12.1	14.5	10 09.7	14.2	56.3
16	60 47.3	43.1	114 45.6	14.5	9 55.5	14.3	56.2
17	75 47.3	43.9	129 19.1	14.5	9 41.2	14.2	56.2
18	90 47.4	N15 44.6	143 52.6	14.7	S 9 27.0	14.3	56.2
19	105 47.5	45.3	158 26.3	14.7	9 12.7	14.3	56.2
20	120 47.5	46.1	173 00.0	14.7	8 58.4	14.3	56.1
21	135 47.6	.. 46.8	187 33.7	14.9	8 44.1	14.4	56.1
22	150 47.7	47.5	202 07.6	14.8	8 29.7	14.4	56.1
23	165 47.7	48.3	216 41.4	15.0	8 15.3	14.4	56.1
	S.D. 15.9	d 0.7	S.D. 15.7		15.5		15.3

Twilight / Sunrise / Moonrise

Lat.	Naut.	Civil	Sunrise	1	2	3	4
N 72	////	////	01 47	■	06 28	04 56	04 13
N 70	////	////	02 27	■	05 25	04 34	04 03
68	////	00 59	02 54	■	04 49	04 17	03 55
66	////	01 51	03 15	04 59	04 23	04 03	03 48
64	////	02 22	03 31	04 19	04 02	03 51	03 42
62	00 52	02 45	03 45	03 51	03 46	03 41	03 37
60	01 39	03 03	03 56	03 29	03 32	03 33	03 32
N 58	02 07	03 17	04 06	03 11	03 20	03 25	03 28
56	02 28	03 30	04 15	02 56	03 10	03 18	03 25
54	02 45	03 41	04 22	02 43	03 00	03 12	03 22
52	03 00	03 50	04 29	02 32	02 52	03 07	03 19
50	03 12	03 59	04 35	02 22	02 45	03 02	03 16
45	03 36	04 16	04 48	02 00	02 29	02 51	03 10
N 40	03 54	04 30	04 59	01 43	02 16	02 42	03 05
35	04 09	04 41	05 09	01 28	02 04	02 35	03 01
30	04 21	04 51	05 17	01 15	01 55	02 28	02 58
20	04 40	05 07	05 30	00 54	01 38	02 16	02 51
N 10	04 55	05 21	05 42	00 34	01 23	02 06	02 45
0	05 07	05 32	05 54	00 17	01 09	01 56	02 40
S 10	05 18	05 43	06 05	24 55	00 55	01 46	02 35
20	05 27	05 53	06 16	24 39	00 39	01 36	02 29
30	05 36	06 05	06 29	24 22	00 22	01 24	02 22
35	05 41	06 11	06 37	24 12	00 12	01 17	02 18
40	05 45	06 17	06 45	24 00	00 00	01 09	02 14
45	05 50	06 25	06 55	23 46	24 59	00 59	02 09
S 50	05 55	06 33	07 08	23 29	24 48	00 48	02 03
52	05 57	06 37	07 13	23 21	24 43	00 43	02 00
54	05 59	06 41	07 19	23 12	24 37	00 37	01 57
56	06 02	06 46	07 26	23 02	24 30	00 30	01 54
58	06 04	06 51	07 34	22 51	24 23	00 23	01 50
S 60	06 07	06 57	07 43	22 37	24 15	00 15	01 46

Sunset / Twilight / Moonset

Lat.	Sunset	Civil	Naut.	1	2	3	4
N 72	22 15	////	////	■	08 36	11 46	14 00
N 70	21 32	////	////	■	09 38	12 05	14 07
68	21 03	23 07	////	■	10 12	12 20	14 12
66	20 42	22 08	////	08 15	10 37	12 33	14 17
64	20 25	21 36	////	08 54	10 56	12 43	14 21
62	20 11	21 12	23 13	09 22	11 11	12 51	14 24
60	19 59	20 54	22 20	09 42	11 24	12 59	14 27
N 58	19 49	20 38	21 50	10 00	11 35	13 05	14 30
56	19 41	20 26	21 28	10 14	11 45	13 11	14 32
54	19 33	20 15	21 11	10 26	11 53	13 16	14 34
52	19 26	20 05	20 56	10 37	12 01	13 20	14 36
50	19 20	19 57	20 44	10 47	12 07	13 24	14 38
45	19 06	19 39	20 19	11 07	12 22	13 33	14 42
N 40	18 55	19 25	20 01	11 23	12 33	13 41	14 45
35	18 46	19 13	19 46	11 37	12 43	13 47	14 47
30	18 38	19 03	19 33	11 48	12 52	13 52	14 50
20	18 24	18 47	19 14	12 09	13 07	14 02	14 54
N 10	18 12	18 34	18 59	12 26	13 20	14 10	14 57
0	18 00	18 22	18 47	12 42	13 32	14 17	15 00
S 10	17 49	18 11	18 36	12 58	13 44	14 25	15 03
20	17 38	18 00	18 27	13 15	13 56	14 33	15 07
30	17 24	17 49	18 17	13 34	14 11	14 42	15 10
35	17 17	17 43	18 13	13 46	14 19	14 47	15 13
40	17 08	17 36	18 08	13 59	14 28	14 53	15 15
45	16 58	17 29	18 04	14 14	14 39	15 00	15 18
S 50	16 46	17 20	17 58	14 32	14 52	15 08	15 21
52	16 40	17 16	17 56	14 41	14 58	15 12	15 23
54	16 34	17 12	17 54	15 01	15 05	15 16	15 24
56	16 27	17 07	17 51	15 01	15 12	15 20	15 26
58	16 19	17 02	17 49	15 14	15 21	15 25	15 28
S 60	16 11	16 56	17 46	15 28	15 31	15 31	15 30

SUN / MOON

Day	SUN Eqn. of Time 00ʰ	12ʰ	Mer. Pass.	MOON Mer. Pass. Upper	Lower	Age	Phase
	m s	m s	h m	h m	h m	d	
1	02 51	02 54	11 57	06 29	18 56	22	
2	02 58	03 01	11 57	07 20	19 44	23	◗
3	03 05	03 08	11 57	08 07	20 29	24	

Table 2. Daily Page from The Nautical Almanac..

14m — INCREMENTS AND CORRECTIONS — 15m

14 (s)	SUN PLANETS ° ′	ARIES ° ′	MOON ° ′	v or Corrn d	v or Corrn d	v or Corrn d
00	3 30·0	3 30·6	3 20·4	0·0 0·0	6·0 1·5	12·0 2·9
01	3 30·3	3 30·8	3 20·7	0·1 0·0	6·1 1·5	12·1 2·9
02	3 30·5	3 31·1	3 20·9	0·2 0·0	6·2 1·5	12·2 2·9
03	3 30·8	3 31·3	3 21·1	0·3 0·1	6·3 1·5	12·3 3·0
04	3 31·0	3 31·6	3 21·4	0·4 0·1	6·4 1·5	12·4 3·0
05	3 31·3	3 31·8	3 21·6	0·5 0·1	6·5 1·6	12·5 3·0
06	3 31·5	3 32·1	3 21·9	0·6 0·1	6·6 1·6	12·6 3·0
07	3 31·8	3 32·3	3 22·1	0·7 0·2	6·7 1·6	12·7 3·1
08	3 32·0	3 32·6	3 22·3	0·8 0·2	6·8 1·6	12·8 3·1
09	3 32·3	3 32·8	3 22·6	0·9 0·2	6·9 1·7	12·9 3·1
10	3 32·5	3 33·1	3 22·8	1·0 0·2	7·0 1·7	13·0 3·1
11	3 32·8	3 33·3	3 23·1	1·1 0·3	7·1 1·7	13·1 3·2
12	3 33·0	3 33·6	3 23·3	1·2 0·3	7·2 1·7	13·2 3·2
13	3 33·3	3 33·8	3 23·5	1·3 0·3	7·3 1·8	13·3 3·2
14	3 33·5	3 34·1	3 23·8	1·4 0·3	7·4 1·8	13·4 3·2
15	3 33·8	3 34·3	3 24·0	1·5 0·4	7·5 1·8	13·5 3·3
16	3 34·0	3 34·6	3 24·3	1·6 0·4	7·6 1·8	13·6 3·3
17	3 34·3	3 34·8	3 24·5	1·7 0·4	7·7 1·9	13·7 3·3
18	3 34·5	3 35·1	3 24·7	1·8 0·4	7·8 1·9	13·8 3·3
19	3 34·8	3 35·3	3 25·0	1·9 0·5	7·9 1·9	13·9 3·4
20	3 35·0	3 35·6	3 25·2	2·0 0·5	8·0 1·9	14·0 3·4
21	3 35·3	3 35·8	3 25·4	2·1 0·5	8·1 2·0	14·1 3·4
22	3 35·5	3 36·1	3 25·7	2·2 0·5	8·2 2·0	14·2 3·4
23	3 35·8	3 36·3	3 25·9	2·3 0·6	8·3 2·0	14·3 3·5
24	3 36·0	3 36·6	3 26·2	2·4 0·6	8·4 2·0	14·4 3·5
25	3 36·3	3 36·8	3 26·4	2·5 0·6	8·5 2·1	14·5 3·5
26	3 36·5	3 37·1	3 26·6	2·6 0·6	8·6 2·1	14·6 3·5
27	3 36·8	3 37·3	3 26·9	2·7 0·7	8·7 2·1	14·7 3·6
28	3 37·0	3 37·6	3 27·1	2·8 0·7	8·8 2·1	14·8 3·6
29	3 37·3	3 37·8	3 27·4	2·9 0·7	8·9 2·2	14·9 3·6
30	3 37·5	3 38·1	3 27·6	3·0 0·7	9·0 2·2	15·0 3·6
31	3 37·8	3 38·3	3 27·8	3·1 0·7	9·1 2·2	15·1 3·6
32	3 38·0	3 38·6	3 28·1	3·2 0·8	9·2 2·2	15·2 3·7
33	3 38·3	3 38·8	3 28·3	3·3 0·8	9·3 2·2	15·3 3·7
34	3 38·5	3 39·1	3 28·5	3·4 0·8	9·4 2·3	15·4 3·7
35	3 38·8	3 39·3	3 28·8	3·5 0·8	9·5 2·3	15·5 3·7
36	3 39·0	3 39·6	3 29·0	3·6 0·9	9·6 2·3	15·6 3·8
37	3 39·3	3 39·9	3 29·3	3·7 0·9	9·7 2·3	15·7 3·8
38	3 39·5	3 40·1	3 29·5	3·8 0·9	9·8 2·4	15·8 3·8
39	3 39·8	3 40·4	3 29·7	3·9 0·9	9·9 2·4	15·9 3·8
40	3 40·0	3 40·6	3 30·0	4·0 1·0	10·0 2·4	16·0 3·9
41	3 40·3	3 40·9	3 30·2	4·1 1·0	10·1 2·4	16·1 3·9
42	3 40·5	3 41·1	3 30·5	4·2 1·0	10·2 2·5	16·2 3·9
43	3 40·8	3 41·4	3 30·7	4·3 1·0	10·3 2·5	16·3 3·9
44	3 41·0	3 41·6	3 30·9	4·4 1·1	10·4 2·5	16·4 4·0
45	3 41·3	3 41·9	3 31·2	4·5 1·1	10·5 2·5	16·5 4·0
46	3 41·5	3 42·1	3 31·4	4·6 1·1	10·6 2·6	16·6 4·0
47	3 41·8	3 42·4	3 31·6	4·7 1·1	10·7 2·6	16·7 4·0
48	3 42·0	3 42·6	3 31·9	4·8 1·2	10·8 2·6	16·8 4·1
49	3 42·3	3 42·9	3 32·1	4·9 1·2	10·9 2·6	16·9 4·1
50	3 42·5	3 43·1	3 32·4	5·0 1·2	11·0 2·7	17·0 4·1
51	3 42·8	3 43·4	3 32·6	5·1 1·2	11·1 2·7	17·1 4·1
52	3 43·0	3 43·6	3 32·8	5·2 1·3	11·2 2·7	17·2 4·2
53	3 43·3	3 43·9	3 33·1	5·3 1·3	11·3 2·7	17·3 4·2
54	3 43·5	3 44·1	3 33·3	5·4 1·3	11·4 2·8	17·4 4·2
55	3 43·8	3 44·4	3 33·6	5·5 1·3	11·5 2·8	17·5 4·2
56	3 44·0	3 44·6	3 33·8	5·6 1·4	11·6 2·8	17·6 4·3
57	3 44·3	3 44·9	3 34·0	5·7 1·4	11·7 2·8	17·7 4·3
58	3 44·5	3 45·1	3 34·3	5·8 1·4	11·8 2·9	17·8 4·3
59	3 44·8	3 45·4	3 34·5	5·9 1·4	11·9 2·9	17·9 4·3
60	3 45·0	3 45·6	3 34·8	6·0 1·5	12·0 2·9	18·0 4·4

15 (s)	SUN PLANETS ° ′	ARIES ° ′	MOON ° ′	v or Corrn d	v or Corrn d	v or Corrn d
00	3 45·0	3 45·6	3 34·8	0·0 0·0	6·0 1·6	12·0 3·1
01	3 45·3	3 45·9	3 35·0	0·1 0·0	6·1 1·6	12·1 3·1
02	3 45·5	3 46·1	3 35·2	0·2 0·1	6·2 1·6	12·2 3·2
03	3 45·8	3 46·4	3 35·5	0·3 0·1	6·3 1·6	12·3 3·2
04	3 46·0	3 46·6	3 35·7	0·4 0·1	6·4 1·7	12·4 3·2
05	3 46·3	3 46·9	3 35·9	0·5 0·1	6·5 1·7	12·5 3·2
06	3 46·5	3 47·1	3 36·2	0·6 0·2	6·6 1·7	12·6 3·3
07	3 46·8	3 47·4	3 36·4	0·7 0·2	6·7 1·7	12·7 3·3
08	3 47·0	3 47·6	3 36·7	0·8 0·2	6·8 1·8	12·8 3·3
09	3 47·3	3 47·9	3 36·9	0·9 0·2	6·9 1·8	12·9 3·3
10	3 47·5	3 48·1	3 37·1	1·0 0·3	7·0 1·8	13·0 3·4
11	3 47·8	3 48·4	3 37·4	1·1 0·3	7·1 1·8	13·1 3·4
12	3 48·0	3 48·6	3 37·6	1·2 0·3	7·2 1·9	13·2 3·4
13	3 48·3	3 48·9	3 37·9	1·3 0·3	7·3 1·9	13·3 3·4
14	3 48·5	3 49·1	3 38·1	1·4 0·4	7·4 1·9	13·4 3·5
15	3 48·8	3 49·4	3 38·3	1·5 0·4	7·5 1·9	13·5 3·5
16	3 49·0	3 49·6	3 38·6	1·6 0·4	7·6 2·0	13·6 3·5
17	3 49·3	3 49·9	3 38·8	1·7 0·4	7·7 2·0	13·7 3·5
18	3 49·5	3 50·1	3 39·0	1·8 0·5	7·8 2·0	13·8 3·6
19	3 49·8	3 50·4	3 39·3	1·9 0·5	7·9 2·0	13·9 3·6
20	3 50·0	3 50·6	3 39·5	2·0 0·5	8·0 2·1	14·0 3·6
21	3 50·3	3 50·9	3 39·8	2·1 0·5	8·1 2·1	14·1 3·6
22	3 50·5	3 51·1	3 40·0	2·2 0·6	8·2 2·1	14·2 3·7
23	3 50·8	3 51·4	3 40·2	2·3 0·6	8·3 2·1	14·3 3·7
24	3 51·0	3 51·6	3 40·5	2·4 0·6	8·4 2·2	14·4 3·7
25	3 51·3	3 51·9	3 40·7	2·5 0·6	8·5 2·2	14·5 3·7
26	3 51·5	3 52·1	3 41·0	2·6 0·7	8·6 2·2	14·6 3·8
27	3 51·8	3 52·4	3 41·2	2·7 0·7	8·7 2·2	14·7 3·8
28	3 52·0	3 52·6	3 41·4	2·8 0·7	8·8 2·3	14·8 3·8
29	3 52·3	3 52·9	3 41·7	2·9 0·7	8·9 2·3	14·9 3·8
30	3 52·5	3 53·1	3 41·9	3·0 0·8	9·0 2·3	15·0 3·9
31	3 52·8	3 53·4	3 42·1	3·1 0·8	9·1 2·4	15·1 3·9
32	3 53·0	3 53·6	3 42·4	3·2 0·8	9·2 2·4	15·2 3·9
33	3 53·3	3 53·9	3 42·6	3·3 0·9	9·3 2·4	15·3 4·0
34	3 53·5	3 54·1	3 42·9	3·4 0·9	9·4 2·4	15·4 4·0
35	3 53·8	3 54·4	3 43·1	3·5 0·9	9·5 2·5	15·5 4·0
36	3 54·0	3 54·6	3 43·3	3·6 0·9	9·6 2·5	15·6 4·0
37	3 54·3	3 54·9	3 43·6	3·7 1·0	9·7 2·5	15·7 4·1
38	3 54·5	3 55·1	3 43·8	3·8 1·0	9·8 2·5	15·8 4·1
39	3 54·8	3 55·4	3 44·1	3·9 1·0	9·9 2·6	15·9 4·1
40	3 55·0	3 55·6	3 44·3	4·0 1·0	10·0 2·6	16·0 4·1
41	3 55·3	3 55·9	3 44·5	4·1 1·1	10·1 2·6	16·1 4·2
42	3 55·5	3 56·1	3 44·8	4·2 1·1	10·2 2·6	16·2 4·2
43	3 55·8	3 56·4	3 45·0	4·3 1·1	10·3 2·7	16·3 4·2
44	3 56·0	3 56·6	3 45·2	4·4 1·1	10·4 2·7	16·4 4·2
45	3 56·3	3 56·9	3 45·5	4·5 1·2	10·5 2·7	16·5 4·3
46	3 56·5	3 57·1	3 45·7	4·6 1·2	10·6 2·7	16·6 4·3
47	3 56·8	3 57·4	3 46·0	4·7 1·2	10·7 2·8	16·7 4·3
48	3 57·0	3 57·6	3 46·2	4·8 1·2	10·8 2·8	16·8 4·3
49	3 57·3	3 57·9	3 46·4	4·9 1·3	10·9 2·8	16·9 4·4
50	3 57·5	3 58·2	3 46·7	5·0 1·3	11·0 2·8	17·0 4·4
51	3 57·8	3 58·4	3 46·9	5·1 1·3	11·1 2·9	17·1 4·4
52	3 58·0	3 58·7	3 47·2	5·2 1·3	11·2 2·9	17·2 4·4
53	3 58·3	3 58·9	3 47·4	5·3 1·4	11·3 2·9	17·3 4·5
54	3 58·5	3 59·2	3 47·6	5·4 1·4	11·4 2·9	17·4 4·5
55	3 58·8	3 59·4	3 47·9	5·5 1·4	11·5 3·0	17·5 4·5
56	3 59·0	3 59·7	3 48·1	5·6 1·4	11·6 3·0	17·6 4·5
57	3 59·3	3 59·9	3 48·4	5·7 1·5	11·7 3·0	17·7 4·6
58	3 59·5	4 00·2	3 48·6	5·8 1·5	11·8 3·0	17·8 4·6
59	3 59·8	4 00·4	3 48·8	5·9 1·5	11·9 3·1	17·9 4·6
60	4 00·0	4 00·7	3 49·1	6·0 1·6	12·0 3·1	18·0 4·7

Table 3. An increment (yellow) page from The Nautical Almanac..

16ᵐ INCREMENTS AND CORRECTIONS 17ᵐ

16	SUN PLANETS	ARIES	MOON	v or Corrn d	v or Corrn d	v or Corrn d
s	° ′	° ′	° ′	′ ′	′ ′	′ ′
00	4 00·0	4 00·7	3 49·1	0·0 0·0	6·0 1·7	12·0 3·3
01	4 00·3	4 00·9	3 49·3	0·1 0·0	6·1 1·7	12·1 3·3
02	4 00·5	4 01·2	3 49·5	0·2 0·1	6·2 1·7	12·2 3·4
03	4 00·8	4 01·4	3 49·8	0·3 0·1	6·3 1·7	12·3 3·4
04	4 01·0	4 01·7	3 50·0	0·4 0·1	6·4 1·8	12·4 3·4
05	4 01·3	4 01·9	3 50·3	0·5 0·1	6·5 1·8	12·5 3·4
06	4 01·5	4 02·2	3 50·5	0·6 0·2	6·6 1·8	12·6 3·5
07	4 01·8	4 02·4	3 50·7	0·7 0·2	6·7 1·8	12·7 3·5
08	4 02·0	4 02·7	3 51·0	0·8 0·2	6·8 1·9	12·8 3·5
09	4 02·3	4 02·9	3 51·2	0·9 0·2	6·9 1·9	12·9 3·5
10	4 02·5	4 03·2	3 51·5	1·0 0·3	7·0 1·9	13·0 3·6
11	4 02·8	4 03·4	3 51·7	1·1 0·3	7·1 2·0	13·1 3·6
12	4 03·0	4 03·7	3 51·9	1·2 0·3	7·2 2·0	13·2 3·6
13	4 03·3	4 03·9	3 52·2	1·3 0·4	7·3 2·0	13·3 3·7
14	4 03·5	4 04·2	3 52·4	1·4 0·4	7·4 2·0	13·4 3·7
15	4 03·8	4 04·4	3 52·6	1·5 0·4	7·5 2·1	13·5 3·7
16	4 04·0	4 04·7	3 52·9	1·6 0·4	7·6 2·1	13·6 3·7
17	4 04·3	4 04·9	3 53·1	1·7 0·5	7·7 2·1	13·7 3·8
18	4 04·5	4 05·2	3 53·4	1·8 0·5	7·8 2·1	13·8 3·8
19	4 04·8	4 05·4	3 53·6	1·9 0·5	7·9 2·2	13·9 3·8
20	4 05·0	4 05·7	3 53·8	2·0 0·6	8·0 2·2	14·0 3·9
21	4 05·3	4 05·9	3 54·1	2·1 0·6	8·1 2·2	14·1 3·9
22	4 05·5	4 06·2	3 54·3	2·2 0·6	8·2 2·3	14·2 3·9
23	4 05·8	4 06·4	3 54·6	2·3 0·6	8·3 2·3	14·3 3·9
24	4 06·0	4 06·7	3 54·8	2·4 0·7	8·4 2·3	14·4 4·0
25	4 06·3	4 06·9	3 55·0	2·5 0·7	8·5 2·3	14·5 4·0
26	4 06·5	4 07·2	3 55·3	2·6 0·7	8·6 2·4	14·6 4·0
27	4 06·8	4 07·4	3 55·5	2·7 0·7	8·7 2·4	14·7 4·0
28	4 07·0	4 07·7	3 55·7	2·8 0·8	8·8 2·4	14·8 4·1
29	4 07·3	4 07·9	3 56·0	2·9 0·8	8·9 2·4	14·9 4·1
30	4 07·5	4 08·2	3 56·2	3·0 0·8	9·0 2·5	15·0 4·1
31	4 07·8	4 08·4	3 56·5	3·1 0·9	9·1 2·5	15·1 4·2
32	4 08·0	4 08·7	3 56·7	3·2 0·9	9·2 2·5	15·2 4·2
33	4 08·3	4 08·9	3 56·9	3·3 0·9	9·3 2·6	15·3 4·2
34	4 08·5	4 09·2	3 57·2	3·4 0·9	9·4 2·6	15·4 4·2
35	4 08·8	4 09·4	3 57·4	3·5 1·0	9·5 2·6	15·5 4·3
36	4 09·0	4 09·7	3 57·7	3·6 1·0	9·6 2·6	15·6 4·3
37	4 09·3	4 09·9	3 57·9	3·7 1·0	9·7 2·7	15·7 4·3
38	4 09·5	4 10·2	3 58·1	3·8 1·0	9·8 2·7	15·8 4·3
39	4 09·8	4 10·4	3 58·4	3·9 1·1	9·9 2·7	15·9 4·4
40	4 10·0	4 10·7	3 58·6	4·0 1·1	10·0 2·8	16·0 4·4
41	4 10·3	4 10·9	3 58·8	4·1 1·1	10·1 2·8	16·1 4·4
42	4 10·5	4 11·2	3 59·1	4·2 1·2	10·2 2·8	16·2 4·5
43	4 10·8	4 11·4	3 59·3	4·3 1·2	10·3 2·8	16·3 4·5
44	4 11·0	4 11·7	3 59·6	4·4 1·2	10·4 2·9	16·4 4·5
45	4 11·3	4 11·9	3 59·8	4·5 1·2	10·5 2·9	16·5 4·5
46	4 11·5	4 12·2	4 00·0	4·6 1·3	10·6 2·9	16·6 4·6
47	4 11·8	4 12·4	4 00·3	4·7 1·3	10·7 2·9	16·7 4·6
48	4 12·0	4 12·7	4 00·5	4·8 1·3	10·8 3·0	16·8 4·6
49	4 12·3	4 12·9	4 00·8	4·9 1·3	10·9 3·0	16·9 4·6
50	4 12·5	4 13·2	4 01·0	5·0 1·4	11·0 3·0	17·0 4·7
51	4 12·8	4 13·4	4 01·2	5·1 1·4	11·1 3·1	17·1 4·7
52	4 13·0	4 13·7	4 01·5	5·2 1·4	11·2 3·1	17·2 4·7
53	4 13·3	4 13·9	4 01·7	5·3 1·5	11·3 3·1	17·3 4·8
54	4 13·5	4 14·2	4 02·0	5·4 1·5	11·4 3·1	17·4 4·8
55	4 13·8	4 14·4	4 02·2	5·5 1·5	11·5 3·2	17·5 4·8
56	4 14·0	4 14·7	4 02·4	5·6 1·5	11·6 3·2	17·6 4·8
57	4 14·3	4 14·9	4 02·7	5·7 1·6	11·7 3·2	17·7 4·9
58	4 14·5	4 15·2	4 02·9	5·8 1·6	11·8 3·2	17·8 4·9
59	4 14·8	4 15·4	4 03·1	5·9 1·6	11·9 3·3	17·9 4·9
60	4 15·0	4 15·7	4 03·4	6·0 1·7	12·0 3·3	18·0 5·0

17	SUN PLANETS	ARIES	MOON	v or Corrn d	v or Corrn d	v or Corrn d
s	° ′	° ′	° ′	′ ′	′ ′	′ ′
00	4 15·0	4 15·7	4 03·4	0·0 0·0	6·0 1·8	12·0 3·5
01	4 15·3	4 15·9	4 03·6	0·1 0·0	6·1 1·8	12·1 3·5
02	4 15·5	4 16·2	4 03·9	0·2 0·1	6·2 1·8	12·2 3·6
03	4 15·8	4 16·5	4 04·1	0·3 0·1	6·3 1·8	12·3 3·6
04	4 16·0	4 16·7	4 04·3	0·4 0·1	6·4 1·9	12·4 3·6
05	4 16·3	4 17·0	4 04·6	0·5 0·1	6·5 1·9	12·5 3·6
06	4 16·5	4 17·2	4 04·8	0·6 0·2	6·6 1·9	12·6 3·7
07	4 16·8	4 17·5	4 05·1	0·7 0·2	6·7 2·0	12·7 3·7
08	4 17·0	4 17·7	4 05·3	0·8 0·2	6·8 2·0	12·8 3·7
09	4 17·3	4 18·0	4 05·5	0·9 0·3	6·9 2·0	12·9 3·8
10	4 17·5	4 18·2	4 05·8	1·0 0·3	7·0 2·0	13·0 3·8
11	4 17·8	4 18·5	4 06·0	1·1 0·3	7·1 2·1	13·1 3·8
12	4 18·0	4 18·7	4 06·2	1·2 0·4	7·2 2·1	13·2 3·9
13	4 18·3	4 19·0	4 06·5	1·3 0·4	7·3 2·1	13·3 3·9
14	4 18·5	4 19·2	4 06·7	1·4 0·4	7·4 2·2	13·4 3·9
15	4 18·8	4 19·5	4 07·0	1·5 0·4	7·5 2·2	13·5 3·9
16	4 19·0	4 19·7	4 07·2	1·6 0·5	7·6 2·2	13·6 4·0
17	4 19·3	4 20·0	4 07·4	1·7 0·5	7·7 2·2	13·7 4·0
18	4 19·5	4 20·2	4 07·7	1·8 0·5	7·8 2·3	13·8 4·0
19	4 19·8	4 20·5	4 07·9	1·9 0·6	7·9 2·3	13·9 4·1
20	4 20·0	4 20·7	4 08·2	2·0 0·6	8·0 2·3	14·0 4·1
21	4 20·3	4 21·0	4 08·4	2·1 0·6	8·1 2·4	14·1 4·1
22	4 20·5	4 21·2	4 08·6	2·2 0·6	8·2 2·4	14·2 4·1
23	4 20·8	4 21·5	4 08·9	2·3 0·7	8·3 2·4	14·3 4·2
24	4 21·0	4 21·7	4 09·1	2·4 0·7	8·4 2·5	14·4 4·2
25	4 21·3	4 22·0	4 09·3	2·5 0·7	8·5 2·5	14·5 4·2
26	4 21·5	4 22·2	4 09·6	2·6 0·8	8·6 2·5	14·6 4·3
27	4 21·8	4 22·5	4 09·8	2·7 0·8	8·7 2·5	14·7 4·3
28	4 22·0	4 22·7	4 10·1	2·8 0·8	8·8 2·6	14·8 4·3
29	4 22·3	4 23·0	4 10·3	2·9 0·8	8·9 2·6	14·9 4·3
30	4 22·5	4 23·2	4 10·5	3·0 0·9	9·0 2·6	15·0 4·4
31	4 22·8	4 23·5	4 10·8	3·1 0·9	9·1 2·7	15·1 4·4
32	4 23·0	4 23·7	4 11·0	3·2 0·9	9·2 2·7	15·2 4·4
33	4 23·3	4 24·0	4 11·3	3·3 1·0	9·3 2·7	15·3 4·5
34	4 23·5	4 24·2	4 11·5	3·4 1·0	9·4 2·7	15·4 4·5
35	4 23·8	4 24·5	4 11·7	3·5 1·0	9·5 2·8	15·5 4·5
36	4 24·0	4 24·7	4 12·0	3·6 1·1	9·6 2·8	15·6 4·6
37	4 24·3	4 25·0	4 12·2	3·7 1·1	9·7 2·8	15·7 4·6
38	4 24·5	4 25·2	4 12·5	3·8 1·1	9·8 2·9	15·8 4·6
39	4 24·8	4 25·5	4 12·7	3·9 1·1	9·9 2·9	15·9 4·6
40	4 25·0	4 25·7	4 12·9	4·0 1·2	10·0 2·9	16·0 4·7
41	4 25·3	4 26·0	4 13·2	4·1 1·2	10·1 2·9	16·1 4·7
42	4 25·5	4 26·2	4 13·4	4·2 1·2	10·2 3·0	16·2 4·7
43	4 25·8	4 26·5	4 13·6	4·3 1·3	10·3 3·0	16·3 4·8
44	4 26·0	4 26·7	4 13·9	4·4 1·3	10·4 3·0	16·4 4·8
45	4 26·3	4 27·0	4 14·1	4·5 1·3	10·5 3·1	16·5 4·8
46	4 26·5	4 27·2	4 14·4	4·6 1·3	10·6 3·1	16·6 4·8
47	4 26·8	4 27·5	4 14·6	4·7 1·4	10·7 3·1	16·7 4·9
48	4 27·0	4 27·7	4 14·8	4·8 1·4	10·8 3·2	16·8 4·9
49	4 27·3	4 28·0	4 15·1	4·9 1·4	10·9 3·2	16·9 4·9
50	4 27·5	4 28·2	4 15·3	5·0 1·5	11·0 3·2	17·0 5·0
51	4 27·8	4 28·5	4 15·6	5·1 1·5	11·1 3·2	17·1 5·0
52	4 28·0	4 28·7	4 15·8	5·2 1·5	11·2 3·3	17·2 5·0
53	4 28·3	4 29·0	4 16·0	5·3 1·5	11·3 3·3	17·3 5·0
54	4 28·5	4 29·2	4 16·3	5·4 1·6	11·4 3·3	17·4 5·1
55	4 28·8	4 29·5	4 16·5	5·5 1·6	11·5 3·4	17·5 5·1
56	4 29·0	4 29·7	4 16·7	5·6 1·6	11·6 3·4	17·6 5·1
57	4 29·3	4 30·0	4 17·0	5·7 1·7	11·7 3·4	17·7 5·2
58	4 29·5	4 30·2	4 17·2	5·8 1·7	11·8 3·4	17·8 5·2
59	4 29·8	4 30·5	4 17·5	5·9 1·7	11·9 3·5	17·9 5·2
60	4 30·0	4 30·7	4 17·7	6·0 1·8	12·0 3·5	18·0 5·3

x

Table 4. An increment (yellow) page from The Nautical Almanac..

52ᵐ   INCREMENTS AND CORRECTIONS   55ᵐ

52	SUN PLANETS	ARIES	MOON	v or Corrⁿ d	v or Corrⁿ d	v or Corrⁿ d
s	° ′	° ′	° ′	′ ′	′ ′	′ ′
00	13 00·0	13 02·1	12 24·5	0·0 0·0	6·0 5·3	12·0 10·5
01	13 00·3	13 02·4	12 24·7	0·1 0·1	6·1 5·3	12·1 10·6
02	13 00·5	13 02·6	12 24·9	0·2 0·2	6·2 5·4	12·2 10·7
03	13 00·8	13 02·9	12 25·2	0·3 0·3	6·3 5·5	12·3 10·8
04	13 01·0	13 03·1	12 25·4	0·4 0·4	6·4 5·6	12·4 10·9
05	13 01·3	13 03·4	12 25·7	0·5 0·4	6·5 5·7	12·5 10·9
06	13 01·5	13 03·6	12 25·9	0·6 0·5	6·6 5·8	12·6 11·0
07	13 01·8	13 03·9	12 26·1	0·7 0·6	6·7 5·9	12·7 11·1
08	13 02·0	13 04·1	12 26·4	0·8 0·7	6·8 5·9	12·8 11·2
09	13 02·3	13 04·4	12 26·6	0·9 0·8	6·9 6·0	12·9 11·3
10	13 02·5	13 04·6	12 26·9	1·0 0·9	7·0 6·1	13·0 11·4
11	13 02·8	13 04·9	12 27·1	1·1 1·0	7·1 6·2	13·1 11·5
12	13 03·0	13 05·1	12 27·3	1·2 1·1	7·2 6·3	13·2 11·6
13	13 03·3	13 05·4	12 27·6	1·3 1·1	7·3 6·4	13·3 11·6
14	13 03·5	13 05·6	12 27·8	1·4 1·2	7·4 6·5	13·4 11·7
15	13 03·8	13 05·9	12 28·0	1·5 1·3	7·5 6·6	13·5 11·8
16	13 04·0	13 06·1	12 28·3	1·6 1·4	7·6 6·7	13·6 11·9
17	13 04·3	13 06·4	12 28·5	1·7 1·5	7·7 6·7	13·7 12·0
18	13 04·5	13 06·6	12 28·8	1·8 1·6	7·8 6·8	13·8 12·1
19	13 04·8	13 06·9	12 29·0	1·9 1·7	7·9 6·9	13·9 12·2
20	13 05·0	13 07·1	12 29·2	2·0 1·8	8·0 7·0	14·0 12·3
21	13 05·3	13 07·4	12 29·5	2·1 1·8	8·1 7·1	14·1 12·3
22	13 05·5	13 07·7	12 29·7	2·2 1·9	8·2 7·2	14·2 12·4
23	13 05·8	13 07·9	12 30·0	2·3 2·0	8·3 7·3	14·3 12·5
24	13 06·0	13 08·2	12 30·2	2·4 2·1	8·4 7·4	14·4 12·6
25	13 06·3	13 08·4	12 30·4	2·5 2·2	8·5 7·4	14·5 12·7
26	13 06·5	13 08·7	12 30·7	2·6 2·3	8·6 7·5	14·6 12·8
27	13 06·8	13 08·9	12 30·9	2·7 2·4	8·7 7·6	14·7 12·9
28	13 07·0	13 09·2	12 31·1	2·8 2·5	8·8 7·7	14·8 13·0
29	13 07·3	13 09·4	12 31·4	2·9 2·5	8·9 7·8	14·9 13·0
30	13 07·5	13 09·7	12 31·6	3·0 2·6	9·0 7·9	15·0 13·1
31	13 07·8	13 09·9	12 31·9	3·1 2·7	9·1 8·0	15·1 13·2
32	13 08·0	13 10·2	12 32·1	3·2 2·8	9·2 8·1	15·2 13·3
33	13 08·3	13 10·4	12 32·3	3·3 2·9	9·3 8·1	15·3 13·4
34	13 08·5	13 10·7	12 32·6	3·4 3·0	9·4 8·2	15·4 13·5
35	13 08·8	13 10·9	12 32·8	3·5 3·1	9·5 8·3	15·5 13·6
36	13 09·0	13 11·2	12 33·1	3·6 3·2	9·6 8·4	15·6 13·7
37	13 09·3	13 11·4	12 33·3	3·7 3·2	9·7 8·5	15·7 13·7
38	13 09·5	13 11·7	12 33·5	3·8 3·3	9·8 8·6	15·8 13·8
39	13 09·8	13 11·9	12 33·8	3·9 3·4	9·9 8·7	15·9 13·9
40	13 10·0	13 12·2	12 34·0	4·0 3·5	10·0 8·8	16·0 14·0
41	13 10·3	13 12·4	12 34·2	4·1 3·6	10·1 8·8	16·1 14·1
42	13 10·5	13 12·7	12 34·5	4·2 3·7	10·2 8·9	16·2 14·2
43	13 10·8	13 12·9	12 34·7	4·3 3·8	10·3 9·0	16·3 14·3
44	13 11·0	13 13·2	12 35·0	4·4 3·9	10·4 9·1	16·4 14·4
45	13 11·3	13 13·4	12 35·2	4·5 3·9	10·5 9·2	16·5 14·4
46	13 11·5	13 13·7	12 35·4	4·6 4·0	10·6 9·3	16·6 14·5
47	13 11·8	13 13·9	12 35·7	4·7 4·1	10·7 9·4	16·7 14·6
48	13 12·0	13 14·2	12 35·9	4·8 4·2	10·8 9·5	16·8 14·7
49	13 12·3	13 14·4	12 36·2	4·9 4·3	10·9 9·5	16·9 14·8
50	13 12·5	13 14·7	12 36·4	5·0 4·4	11·0 9·6	17·0 14·9
51	13 12·8	13 14·9	12 36·6	5·1 4·5	11·1 9·7	17·1 15·0
52	13 13·0	13 15·2	12 36·9	5·2 4·6	11·2 9·8	17·2 15·1
53	13 13·3	13 15·4	12 37·1	5·3 4·6	11·3 9·9	17·3 15·1
54	13 13·5	13 15·7	12 37·4	5·4 4·7	11·4 10·0	17·4 15·2
55	13 13·8	13 15·9	12 37·6	5·5 4·8	11·5 10·1	17·5 15·3
56	13 14·0	13 16·2	12 37·8	5·6 4·9	11·6 10·2	17·6 15·4
57	13 14·3	13 16·4	12 38·1	5·7 5·0	11·7 10·2	17·7 15·5
58	13 14·5	13 16·7	12 38·3	5·8 5·1	11·8 10·3	17·8 15·6
59	13 14·8	13 16·9	12 38·5	5·9 5·2	11·9 10·4	17·9 15·7
60	13 15·0	13 17·2	12 38·8	6·0 5·3	12·0 10·5	18·0 15·8

55	SUN PLANETS	ARIES	MOON	v or Corrⁿ d	v or Corrⁿ d	v or Corrⁿ d
s	° ′	° ′	° ′	′ ′	′ ′	′ ′
00	13 45·0	13 47·3	13 07·4	0·0 0·0	6·0 5·6	12·0 11·1
01	13 45·3	13 47·5	13 07·7	0·1 0·1	6·1 5·6	12·1 11·2
02	13 45·5	13 47·8	13 07·9	0·2 0·2	6·2 5·7	12·2 11·3
03	13 45·8	13 48·0	13 08·1	0·3 0·3	6·3 5·8	12·3 11·4
04	13 46·0	13 48·3	13 08·4	0·4 0·4	6·4 5·9	12·4 11·5
05	13 46·3	13 48·5	13 08·6	0·5 0·5	6·5 6·0	12·5 11·6
06	13 46·5	13 48·8	13 08·8	0·6 0·6	6·6 6·1	12·6 11·6
07	13 46·8	13 49·0	13 09·1	0·7 0·6	6·7 6·2	12·7 11·7
08	13 47·0	13 49·3	13 09·3	0·8 0·7	6·8 6·3	12·8 11·8
09	13 47·3	13 49·5	13 09·6	0·9 0·8	6·9 6·4	12·9 11·9
10	13 47·5	13 49·8	13 09·8	1·0 0·9	7·0 6·5	13·0 12·0
11	13 47·8	13 50·0	13 10·0	1·1 1·0	7·1 6·6	13·1 12·1
12	13 48·0	13 50·3	13 10·3	1·2 1·1	7·2 6·7	13·2 12·2
13	13 48·3	13 50·5	13 10·5	1·3 1·2	7·3 6·8	13·3 12·3
14	13 48·5	13 50·8	13 10·8	1·4 1·3	7·4 6·8	13·4 12·4
15	13 48·8	13 51·0	13 11·0	1·5 1·4	7·5 6·9	13·5 12·5
16	13 49·0	13 51·3	13 11·2	1·6 1·5	7·6 7·0	13·6 12·6
17	13 49·3	13 51·5	13 11·5	1·7 1·6	7·7 7·1	13·7 12·7
18	13 49·5	13 51·8	13 11·7	1·8 1·7	7·8 7·2	13·8 12·8
19	13 49·8	13 52·0	13 12·0	1·9 1·8	7·9 7·3	13·9 12·9
20	13 50·0	13 52·3	13 12·2	2·0 ·19	8·0 7·4	14·0 13·0
21	13 50·3	13 52·5	13 12·4	2·1 1·9	8·1 7·5	14·1 13·0
22	13 50·5	13 52·8	13 12·7	2·2 2·0	8·2 7·6	14·2 13·1
23	13 50·8	13 53·0	13 12·9	2·3 2·1	8·3 7·7	14·3 13·2
24	13 51·0	13 53·3	13 13·1	2·4 2·2	8·4 7·8	14·4 13·3
25	13 51·3	13 53·5	13 13·4	2·5 2·3	8·5 7·9	14·5 13·4
26	13 51·5	13 53·8	13 13·6	2·6 2·4	8·6 8·0	14·6 13·5
27	13 51·8	13 54·0	13 13·9	2·7 2·5	8·7 8·0	14·7 13·6
28	13 52·0	13 54·3	13 14·1	2·8 2·6	8·8 8·1	14·8 13·7
29	13 52·3	13 54·5	13 14·3	2·9 2·7	8·9 8·2	14·9 13·8
30	13 52·5	13 54·8	13 14·6	3·0 2·8	9·0 8·3	15·0 13·9
31	13 52·8	13 55·0	13 14·8	3·1 2·9	9·1 8·4	15·1 14·0
32	13 53·0	13 55·3	13 15·1	3·2 3·0	9·2 8·5	15·2 14·1
33	13 53·3	13 55·5	13 15·3	3·3 3·1	9·3 8·6	15·3 14·2
34	13 53·5	13 55·8	13 15·5	3·4 3·1	9·4 8·7	15·4 14·2
35	13 53·8	13 56·0	13 15·8	3·5 3·2	9·5 8·8	15·5 14·3
36	13 54·0	13 56·3	13 16·0	3·6 3·3	9·6 8·9	15·6 14·4
37	13 54·3	13 56·5	13 16·2	3·7 3·4	9·7 9·0	15·7 14·5
38	13 54·5	13 56·8	13 16·5	3·8 3·5	9·8 9·1	15·8 14·6
39	13 54·8	13 57·0	13 16·7	3·9 3·6	9·9 9·2	15·9 14·7
40	13 55·0	13 57·3	13 17·0	4·0 3·7	10·0 9·3	16·0 14·8
41	13 55·3	13 57·5	13 17·2	4·1 3·8	10·1 9·3	16·1 14·9
42	13 55·5	13 57·8	13 17·4	4·2 3·9	10·2 9·4	16·2 15·0
43	13 55·8	13 58·0	13 17·7	4·3 4·0	10·3 9·5	16·3 15·1
44	13 56·0	13 58·3	13 17·9	4·4 4·1	10·4 9·6	16·4 15·2
45	13 56·3	13 58·5	13 18·2	4·5 4·2	10·5 9·7	16·5 15·3
46	13 56·5	13 58·8	13 18·4	4·6 4·3	10·6 9·8	16·6 15·4
47	13 56·8	13 59·0	13 18·6	4·7 4·3	10·7 9·9	16·7 15·4
48	13 57·0	13 59·3	13 18·9	4·8 4·4	10·8 10·0	16·8 15·5
49	13 57·3	13 59·5	13 19·1	4·9 4·5	10·9 10·1	16·9 15·6
50	13 57·5	13 59·8	13 19·3	5·0 4·6	11·0 10·2	17·0 15·7
51	13 57·8	14 00·0	13 19·6	5·1 4·7	11·1 10·3	17·1 15·8
52	13 58·0	14 00·3	13 19·8	5·2 4·8	11·2 10·4	17·2 15·9
53	13 58·3	14 00·5	13 20·1	5·3 4·9	11·3 10·5	17·3 16·0
54	13 58·5	14 00·8	13 20·3	5·4 5·0	11·4 10·5	17·4 16·1
55	13 58·8	14 01·0	13 20·5	5·5 5·1	11·5 10·6	17·5 16·2
56	13 59·0	14 01·3	13 20·8	5·6 5·2	11·6 10·7	17·6 16·3
57	13 59·3	14 01·5	13 21·0	5·7 5·3	11·7 10·8	17·7 16·4
58	13 59·5	14 01·8	13 21·3	5·8 5·4	11·8 10·9	17·8 16·5
59	13 59·8	14 02·0	13 21·5	5·9 5·5	11·9 11·0	17·9 16·6
60	14 00·0	14 02·3	13 21·7	6·0 5·6	12·0 11·1	18·0 16·7

Table 5. Increments and corrections from The Nautical Almanac..

A2 ALTITUDE CORRECTION TABLES 10°–90°—SUN, STARS, PLANETS

SUN

OCT.—MAR.			APR.—SEPT.		
App. Alt.	Lower Limb	Upper Limb	App. Alt.	Lower Limb	Upper Limb
9 34	+10.8	−21.5	9 39	+10.6	−21.2
9 45	+10.9	−21.4	9 51	+10.7	−21.1
9 56	+11.0	−21.3	10 03	+10.8	−21.0
10 08	+11.1	−21.2	10 15	+10.9	−20.9
10 21	+11.2	−21.1	10 27	+11.0	−20.8
10 34	+11.3	−21.0	10 40	+11.1	−20.7
10 47	+11.4	−20.9	10 54	+11.2	−20.6
11 01	+11.5	−20.8	11 08	+11.3	−20.5
11 15	+11.6	−20.7	11 23	+11.4	−20.4
11 30	+11.7	−20.6	11 38	+11.5	−20.3
11 46	+11.8	−20.5	11 54	+11.6	−20.2
12 02	+11.9	−20.4	12 10	+11.7	−20.1
12 19	+12.0	−20.3	12 28	+11.8	−20.0
12 37	+12.1	−20.2	12 46	+11.9	−19.9
12 55	+12.2	−20.1	13 05	+12.0	−19.8
13 14	+12.3	−20.0	13 24	+12.1	−19.7
13 35	+12.4	−19.9	13 45	+12.2	−19.6
13 56	+12.5	−19.8	14 07	+12.3	−19.5
14 18	+12.6	−19.7	14 30	+12.4	−19.4
14 42	+12.7	−19.6	14 54	+12.5	−19.3
15 06	+12.8	−19.5	15 19	+12.6	−19.2
15 32	+12.9	−19.4	15 46	+12.7	−19.1
15 59	+13.0	−19.3	16 14	+12.8	−19.0
16 28	+13.1	−19.2	16 44	+12.9	−18.9
16 59	+13.2	−19.1	17 15	+13.0	−18.8
17 32	+13.3	−19.0	17 48	+13.1	−18.7
18 06	+13.4	−18.9	18 24	+13.2	−18.6
18 42	+13.5	−18.8	19 01	+13.3	−18.5
19 21	+13.6	−18.7	19 42	+13.4	−18.4
20 03	+13.7	−18.6	20 25	+13.5	−18.3
20 48	+13.8	−18.5	21 11	+13.6	−18.2
21 35	+13.9	−18.4	22 00	+13.7	−18.1
22 26	+14.0	−18.3	22 54	+13.8	−18.0
23 22	+14.1	−18.2	23 51	+13.9	−17.9
24 21	+14.2	−18.1	24 53	+14.0	−17.8
25 26	+14.3	−18.0	26 00	+14.1	−17.7
26 36	+14.4	−17.9	27 13	+14.2	−17.6
27 52	+14.5	−17.8	28 33	+14.3	−17.5
29 15	+14.6	−17.7	30 00	+14.4	−17.4
30 46	+14.7	−17.6	31 35	+14.5	−17.3
32 26	+14.8	−17.5	33 20	+14.6	−17.2
34 17	+14.9	−17.4	35 17	+14.7	−17.1
36 20	+15.0	−17.3	37 26	+14.8	−17.0
38 36	+15.1	−17.2	39 50	+14.9	−16.9
41 08	+15.2	−17.1	42 31	+15.0	−16.8
43 59	+15.3	−17.0	45 31	+15.1	−16.7
47 10	+15.4	−16.9	48 55	+15.2	−16.6
50 46	+15.5	−16.8	52 44	+15.3	−16.5
54 49	+15.6	−16.7	57 02	+15.4	−16.4
59 23	+15.7	−16.6	61 51	+15.5	−16.3
64 30	+15.8	−16.5	67 17	+15.6	−16.2
70 12	+15.9	−16.4	73 16	+15.7	−16.1
76 26	+16.0	−16.3	79 43	+15.8	−16.0
83 05	+16.1	−16.2	86 32	+15.9	−15.9
90 00			90 00		

STARS AND PLANETS

App. Alt.	Corrn		App. Alt.	Additional Corrn
9 56	−5.3			**1986**
10 08	−5.2			**VENUS**
10 20	−5.1			Jan. 1–July 20
10 33	−5.0		0 '	
10 46	−4.9		60	+0.1
11 00	−4.8			
11 14	−4.7			July 21–Sept. 8
11 29	−4.6		0 '	
11 45	−4.5		41	+0.2
12 01	−4.4		76	+0.1
12 18	−4.3			
12 35	−4.2			Sept. 9–Oct. 1
12 54	−4.1			Dec. 13–Dec. 31
13 13	−4.0		0 '	
13 33	−3.9		34	+0.3
13 54	−3.8		60	+0.2
14 16	−3.7		80	+0.1
14 40	−3.6			
15 04	−3.5			Oct. 2–Oct. 16
15 30	−3.4			Nov. 27–Dec. 12
15 57	−3.3		0 '	
16 26	−3.2		29	+0.4
16 56	−3.1		51	+0.3
17 28	−3.0		68	+0.2
18 02	−2.9		83	+0.1
18 38	−2.8			
19 17	−2.7			Oct. 17–Nov. 26
19 58	−2.6		0 '	
20 42	−2.5		26	+0.5
21 28	−2.4		46	+0.4
22 19	−2.3		60	+0.3
23 13	−2.2		73	+0.2
24 11	−2.1		84	+0.1
25 14	−2.0			
26 22	−1.9			**MARS**
27 36	−1.8			Jan. 1–Apr. 6
28 56	−1.7			Nov. 15–Dec. 31
30 24	−1.6		0 '	
32 00	−1.5		60	+0.1
33 45	−1.4			
35 40	−1.3			Apr. 7–May 25
37 48	−1.2			Sept. 13–Nov. 14
40 08	−1.1		0 '	
42 44	−1.0		41	+0.2
45 36	−0.9		76	+0.1
48 47	−0.8			
52 18	−0.7			May 26–July 1
56 11	−0.6			Aug. 1–Sept. 12
60 28	−0.5		0 '	
65 08	−0.4		34	+0.3
70 11	−0.3		60	+0.2
75 34	−0.2		80	+0.1
81 13	−0.1			
87 03				July 2–July 31
90 00	0.0		0 '	
			29	+0.4
			51	+0.3
			68	+0.2
			83	+0.1

DIP

Ht. of Eye	Corrn	Ht. of Eye	Ht. of Eye	Corrn
m		ft.	m	
2.4	−2.8	8.0	1.0	−1.8
2.6	−2.9	8.6	1.5	−2.2
2.8	−3.0	9.2	2.0	−2.5
3.0	−3.1	9.8	2.5	−2.8
3.2	−3.2	10.5	3.0	−3.0
3.4	−3.3	11.2	See table ←	
3.6	−3.4	11.9	m	
3.8	−3.5	12.6	20	−7.9
4.0	−3.6	13.3	22	−8.3
4.3	−3.7	14.1	24	−8.6
4.5	−3.8	14.9	26	−9.0
4.7	−3.9	15.7	28	−9.3
5.0	−4.0	16.5		
5.2	−4.1	17.4	30	−9.6
5.5	−4.2	18.3	32	−10.0
5.8	−4.3	19.1	34	−10.3
6.1	−4.4	20.1	36	−10.6
6.3	−4.5	21.0	38	−10.8
6.6	−4.6	22.0		
6.9	−4.7	22.9	40	−11.1
7.2	−4.8	23.9	42	−11.4
7.5	−4.9	24.9	44	−11.7
7.9	−5.0	26.0	46	−11.9
8.2	−5.1	27.1	48	−12.2
8.5	−5.2	28.1	ft.	
8.8	−5.3	29.2	2	−1.4
9.2	−5.4	30.4	4	−1.9
9.5	−5.5	31.5	6	−2.4
9.9	−5.6	32.7	8	−2.7
10.3	−5.7	33.9	10	−3.1
10.6	−5.8	35.1	See table ←	
11.0	−5.9	36.3	ft.	
11.4	−6.0	37.6	70	−8.1
11.8	−6.1	38.9	75	−8.4
12.2	−6.2	40.1	80	−8.7
12.6	−6.3	41.5	85	−8.9
13.0	−6.4	42.8	90	−9.2
13.4	−6.5	44.2	95	−9.5
13.8	−6.6	45.5		
14.2	−6.7	46.9	100	−9.7
14.7	−6.8	48.4	105	−9.9
15.1	−6.9	49.8	110	−10.2
15.5	−7.0	51.3	115	−10.4
16.0	−7.1	52.8	120	−10.6
16.5	−7.2	54.3	125	−10.8
16.9	−7.3	55.8		
17.4	−7.4	57.4	130	−11.1
17.9	−7.5	58.9	135	−11.3
18.4	−7.6	60.5	140	−11.5
18.8	−7.7	62.1	145	−11.7
19.3	−7.8	63.8	150	−11.9
19.8	−7.9	65.4	155	−12.1
20.4	−8.0	67.1		
20.9	−8.1	68.8		
21.4		70.5		

App. Alt. = Apparent altitude = Sextant altitude corrected for index error and dip.

Table 6. 'Bookmark' from The Nautical Almanac..

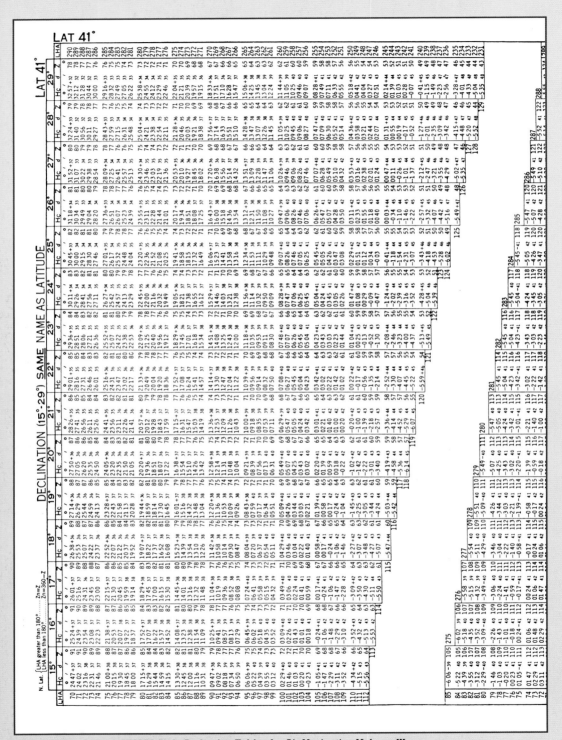

Table 7. A page from AP3270 Sight Reduction Tables for Air Navigation Volume III.

LAT 49°

DECLINATION (15°–29°) SAME NAME AS LATITUDE

Table 8. A page from AP3270 Sight Reduction Tables for Air Navigation Volume III.

TABLE 5.—Correction to Tabulated Altitude for Minutes of Declination

Table 9. Bookmark and inside back cover of AP3270 Volume II and III.

LAT 10°S

LHA ♈	Hc Zn	Hc Zn	Hc Zn	Hc Zn	Hc Zn	Hc Zn	Hc Zn
	•Alpheratz	Hamal	ALDEBARAN	•RIGEL	ACHERNAR	•FOMALHAUT	Enif
0	50 57 003	44 31 042	17 01 069	12 42 096	39 07 163	65 23 215	50 41 299
1	50 59 001	45 10 041	17 57 069	13 41 096	39 24 164	64 49 216	49 49 298
2	51 00 000	45 49 041	18 52 069	14 40 096	39 40 165	64 14 218	48 57 298
3	50 59 358	46 27 040	19 47 068	15 39 096	39 55 165	63 37 219	48 05 297
4	50 56 357	47 04 039	20 42 068	16 37 096	40 10 166	62 59 220	47 12 296
5	50 53 356	47 41 038	21 36 068	17 36 096	40 24 166	62 21 222	46 19 296
6	50 48 354	48 16 037	22 31 067	18 35 095	40 38 167	61 41 223	45 25 295
7	50 41 353	48 51 035	23 25 067	19 34 095	40 50 168	61 00 224	44 32 295
8	50 33 352	49 25 034	24 20 067	20 33 095	41 03 168	60 19 225	43 38 294
9	50 24 350	49 58 033	25 14 066	21 31 095	41 14 169	59 37 226	42 44 293
10	50 13 349	50 30 032	26 08 066	22 30 095	41 25 170	58 54 227	41 50 293
11	50 01 348	51 00 031	27 02 066	23 29 095	41 35 170	58 10 228	40 55 292
12	49 48 346	51 30 030	27 56 065	24 28 095	41 45 171	57 26 229	40 00 292
13	49 33 345	51 59 028	28 49 065	25 27 094	41 53 172	56 41 230	39 05 291
14	49 17 344	52 26 027	29 42 064	26 26 094	42 01 173	55 56 230	38 10 291
	Hamal	ALDEBARAN	•RIGEL	ACHERNAR	•FOMALHAUT	Enif	•Alpheratz
15	52 53 026	30 36 064	27 25 094	42 09 173	55 10 231	37 15 291	49 00 342
16	53 18 024	31 29 064	28 24 094	42 15 174	54 24 232	36 20 290	48 41 341
17	53 41 023	32 21 063	29 23 094	42 21 175	53 37 232	35 24 290	48 22 340
18	54 04 022	33 14 063	30 22 094	42 26 175	52 50 233	34 28 289	48 01 339
19	54 25 020	34 06 062	31 21 094	42 31 176	52 03 234	33 33 289	47 39 338
20	54 44 019	34 58 062	32 20 093	42 34 177	51 15 234	32 37 289	47 16 336
21	55 02 017	35 50 061	33 19 093	42 37 178	50 27 235	31 41 288	46 51 335
22	55 19 016	36 42 061	34 18 093	42 39 178	49 38 235	30 44 288	46 26 334
23	55 34 014	37 33 060	35 17 093	42 41 179	48 50 236	29 48 287	46 00 333
24	55 48 012	38 24 060	36 16 093	42 41 180	48 01 236	28 52 287	45 33 332
25	56 00 011	39 15 059	37 15 093	42 41 181	47 12 237	27 55 287	45 04 331
26	56 10 009	40 06 058	38 14 093	42 40 181	46 22 237	26 59 286	44 35 330
27	56 19 008	40 56 058	39 13 092	42 38 182	45 32 237	26 02 286	44 05 329
28	56 25 006	41 46 057	40 12 092	42 36 183	44 43 238	25 05 286	43 34 328
29	56 31 004	42 35 056	41 11 092	42 33 183	43 52 238	24 08 286	43 02 327
	CAPELLA	•BETELGEUSE	SIRIUS	CANOPUS	•ACHERNAR	FOMALHAUT	•Alpheratz
30	18 58 034	29 07 076	20 48 104	22 27 143	42 29 184	43 02 238	42 30 326
31	19 31 033	30 04 075	21 45 104	23 02 143	42 24 185	42 12 239	41 56 325
32	20 03 033	31 01 075	22 43 104	23 37 144	42 19 186	41 21 239	41 22 324
33	20 34 032	31 58 075	23 40 104	24 12 144	42 13 186	40 31 239	40 47 323
34	21 06 032	32 55 074	24 37 104	24 47 144	42 06 187	39 40 240	40 12 323
35	21 36 031	33 52 074	25 35 104	25 22 144	41 58 188	38 49 240	39 36 322
36	22 07 031	34 49 074	26 32 104	25 56 144	41 50 188	37 58 240	38 59 321
37	22 37 030	35 45 073	27 29 104	26 31 145	41 41 189	37 06 240	38 21 320
38	23 06 030	36 42 073	28 27 104	27 05 145	41 31 190	36 15 240	37 43 319
39	23 35 029	37 38 072	29 24 104	27 39 145	41 21 191	35 24 241	37 04 319
40	24 04 029	38 35 072	30 22 104	28 13 145	41 09 191	34 32 241	36 25 318
41	24 32 028	39 31 072	31 19 104	28 46 146	40 58 192	33 41 241	35 45 317
42	24 59 027	40 27 071	32 17 104	29 20 146	40 45 193	32 49 241	35 04 317
43	25 26 027	41 23 071	33 14 103	29 53 146	40 32 193	31 57 241	34 23 316
44	25 52 026	42 18 070	34 11 103	30 26 146	40 18 194	31 05 241	33 42 315
	CAPELLA	•BETELGEUSE	SIRIUS	CANOPUS	•ACHERNAR	FOMALHAUT	•Alpheratz
45	26 18 026	43 14 070	35 09 103	30 58 147	40 04 194	30 14 241	33 00 315
46	26 44 025	44 09 069	36 06 103	31 30 147	39 49 195	29 22 241	32 18 314
47	27 08 024	45 04 069	37 04 103	32 02 147	39 33 196	28 30 242	31 35 313
48	27 32 024	45 59 068	38 01 103	32 34 148	39 17 196	27 38 242	30 52 313
49	27 56 023	46 54 068	38 59 103	33 05 148	39 00 197	26 46 242	30 08 312
50	28 19 022	47 49 067	39 56 103	33 36 148	38 42 197	25 54 242	29 24 312
51	28 41 022	48 43 066	40 54 103	34 07 149	38 24 198	25 02 242	28 40 311
52	29 02 021	49 37 066	41 51 104	34 38 149	38 06 199	24 10 242	27 55 311
53	29 23 020	50 31 065	42 49 104	35 08 150	37 47 199	23 18 242	27 10 310
54	29 44 020	51 24 064	43 46 104	35 37 150	37 27 200	22 26 242	26 25 310
55	30 03 019	52 18 064	44 44 104	36 06 151	37 07 200	21 33 242	25 39 309
56	30 22 018	53 10 063	45 41 104	36 35 151	36 46 201	20 41 242	24 53 309
57	30 40 018	54 03 062	46 38 104	37 04 152	36 25 201	19 49 242	24 07 308
58	30 58 017	54 55 061	47 36 104	37 32 152	36 03 202	18 57 242	23 20 308
59	31 14 016	55 47 061	48 33 104	37 59 152	35 41 202	18 05 242	22 34 307
	•CAPELLA	POLLUX	•SIRIUS	CANOPUS	ACHERNAR	•Diphda	Hamal
60	31 30 015	23 46 053	49 30 104	38 26 153	35 19 203	41 39 255	46 33 321
61	31 45 015	24 33 053	50 28 104	38 53 154	34 56 203	40 42 255	45 55 320
62	32 00 014	25 20 052	51 25 104	39 19 154	34 32 204	39 45 255	45 17 319
63	32 14 013	26 07 052	52 22 104	39 44 155	34 08 204	38 48 255	44 37 318
64	32 26 012	26 53 051	53 19 105	40 09 155	33 44 205	37 51 255	43 57 317
65	32 39 011	27 39 051	54 17 105	40 34 156	33 19 205	36 54 255	43 16 316
66	32 50 011	28 24 050	55 14 105	40 58 156	32 54 205	35 57 255	42 35 315
67	33 00 010	29 10 050	56 11 105	41 21 157	32 29 206	34 59 255	41 53 314
68	33 10 009	29 55 049	57 08 105	41 44 158	32 03 206	34 02 255	41 11 314
69	33 19 008	30 39 049	58 05 106	42 06 158	31 37 206	33 05 255	40 28 313
70	33 27 007	31 24 048	59 02 106	42 28 159	31 10 207	32 08 255	39 44 312
71	33 34 007	32 07 048	59 58 106	42 49 160	30 43 207	31 11 255	39 00 311
72	33 40 006	32 51 047	60 55 106	43 09 160	30 16 208	30 14 255	38 15 311
73	33 46 005	33 34 046	61 52 107	43 28 161	29 48 208	29 17 255	37 30 310
74	33 51 004	34 16 046	62 48 107	43 47 162	29 21 208	28 20 255	36 45 309
	CAPELLA	POLLUX	•REGULUS	CANOPUS	•ACHERNAR	Diphda	•Hamal
75	33 54 003	34 58 045	10 30 076	44 05 162	28 53 209	27 23 255	35 59 309
76	33 57 002	35 40 044	11 27 075	44 23 163	28 24 209	26 26 255	35 13 308
77	33 59 002	36 21 044	12 24 075	44 39 164	27 56 209	25 29 255	34 26 308
78	34 01 001	37 02 043	13 21 075	44 55 165	27 27 209	24 32 255	33 39 307
79	34 01 000	37 42 042	14 18 075	45 11 166	26 58 210	23 35 255	32 52 306
80	34 00 359	38 21 042	15 15 074	45 25 166	26 28 210	22 38 254	32 04 306
81	33 59 358	39 00 041	16 12 074	45 39 167	25 59 210	21 41 254	31 16 305
82	33 57 357	39 38 040	17 09 074	45 51 168	25 29 210	20 45 254	30 28 305
83	33 54 357	40 16 039	18 06 074	46 03 169	24 59 211	19 48 254	29 39 304
84	33 50 356	40 53 038	19 02 073	46 14 170	24 29 211	18 51 254	28 50 304
85	33 45 355	41 29 037	19 59 073	46 25 170	23 59 211	17 54 254	28 01 303
86	33 39 354	42 05 037	20 56 073	46 34 171	23 28 211	16 57 254	27 12 303
87	33 33 353	42 40 036	21 52 073	46 42 172	22 57 211	16 00 254	26 22 303
88	33 25 352	43 14 035	22 48 072	46 50 173	22 26 212	15 04 254	25 32 302
89	33 17 352	43 47 034	23 45 072	46 57 174	21 55 212	14 07 254	24 42 302

LAT 10°S

LHA ♈	Hc Zn	Hc Zn	Hc Zn	Hc Zn	Hc Zn	Hc Zn	Hc Zn
	POLLUX	•REGULUS	Suhail	•CANOPUS	Acamar	•ALDEBARAN	CAPELLA
90	44 19 033	24 41 072	37 30 138	47 03 175	39 37 225	56 12 321	33 08 351
91	44 51 032	25 37 071	38 09 138	47 08 176	38 55 225	55 34 320	32 58 350
92	45 22 031	26 33 071	38 48 139	47 12 177	38 13 226	54 56 319	32 48 349
93	45 52 030	27 29 071	39 27 139	47 15 177	37 31 226	54 17 318	32 36 348
94	46 21 029	28 24 070	40 05 140	47 17 178	36 48 226	53 36 316	32 24 348
95	46 48 028	29 20 070	40 43 140	47 18 179	36 05 227	52 55 315	32 11 347
96	47 15 027	30 15 070	41 21 141	47 19 180	35 22 227	52 13 314	31 57 346
97	47 41 025	31 11 069	41 58 141	47 18 181	34 39 227	51 31 313	31 42 345
98	48 06 024	32 06 069	42 35 142	47 17 182	33 55 228	50 47 312	31 27 345
99	48 30 023	33 01 068	43 11 142	47 14 183	33 11 228	50 03 311	31 11 344
100	48 52 022	33 56 068	43 47 143	47 11 184	32 27 228	49 18 310	30 54 343
101	49 14 021	34 50 068	44 23 143	47 07 185	31 43 228	48 33 309	30 36 342
102	49 34 019	35 45 067	44 58 144	47 02 185	30 59 229	47 47 309	30 18 342
103	49 53 018	36 39 067	45 32 145	46 56 186	30 15 229	47 01 308	29 59 341
104	50 11 017	37 34 066	46 06 145	46 49 187	29 30 229	46 14 307	29 39 340
	POLLUX	•REGULUS	Suhail	•CANOPUS	RIGEL	•ALDEBARAN	CAPELLA
105	50 27 015	38 28 066	46 39 146	46 41 188	63 44 272	45 26 306	29 19 339
106	50 42 014	39 21 065	47 12 147	46 32 189	62 45 271	44 38 305	28 58 339
107	50 56 013	40 15 065	47 44 147	46 23 190	61 46 271	43 50 305	28 36 338
108	51 08 011	41 08 064	48 16 148	46 12 191	60 47 271	43 01 304	28 14 337
109	51 19 010	42 01 064	48 47 149	46 01 191	59 48 271	42 12 303	27 51 337
110	51 29 009	42 54 063	49 17 150	45 49 192	58 49 271	41 22 303	27 27 336
111	51 37 007	43 47 062	49 46 151	45 36 193	57 50 270	40 32 302	27 03 336
112	51 44 006	44 39 062	50 15 151	45 22 194	56 51 270	39 42 301	26 38 335
113	51 49 004	45 31 061	50 43 152	45 08 195	55 51 270	38 51 301	26 13 334
114	51 53 003	46 22 061	51 10 153	44 52 195	54 52 270	38 00 300	25 47 334
115	51 55 002	47 14 060	51 36 154	44 36 196	53 53 270	37 09 300	25 20 333
116	51 56 000	48 05 059	52 01 155	44 19 197	52 54 270	36 18 299	24 53 332
117	51 56 359	48 55 058	52 25 156	44 02 198	51 55 269	35 26 299	24 26 332
118	51 54 357	49 45 058	52 49 157	43 44 198	50 56 269	34 34 298	23 58 331
119	51 50 356	50 35 057	53 11 158	43 25 199	49 57 269	33 42 298	23 29 331
	•REGULUS	SPICA	•ACRUX	CANOPUS	RIGEL	•BETELGEUSE	POLLUX
120	51 24 056	10 32 100	19 28 154	43 05 200	48 58 269	54 12 298	51 45 354
121	52 13 055	11 31 099	19 54 154	42 45 200	47 59 269	53 20 297	51 39 353
122	53 01 054	12 29 099	20 20 154	42 24 201	47 00 269	52 27 296	51 31 352
123	53 48 053	13 27 099	20 46 154	42 02 202	46 01 268	51 34 296	51 21 350
124	54 35 052	14 26 099	21 12 154	41 40 202	45 02 268	50 41 295	51 11 349
125	55 22 051	15 24 099	21 37 155	41 17 203	44 03 268	49 47 294	50 58 347
126	56 07 050	16 22 099	22 02 155	40 53 204	43 03 268	48 53 294	50 45 346
127	56 52 049	17 21 099	22 27 155	40 29 204	42 04 268	47 59 293	50 30 345
128	57 36 048	18 19 098	22 52 155	40 05 205	41 05 268	47 04 292	50 14 343
129	58 20 046	19 18 098	23 17 155	39 40 205	40 06 268	46 09 292	49 57 342
130	59 02 045	20 16 098	23 41 156	39 14 206	39 07 267	45 14 291	49 38 341
131	59 43 044	21 15 098	24 06 156	38 48 207	38 08 267	44 19 291	49 18 340
132	60 24 042	22 13 098	24 30 156	38 21 207	37 09 267	43 24 290	48 57 338
133	61 03 041	23 12 098	24 54 156	37 54 208	36 10 267	42 28 290	48 34 337
134	61 41 039	24 10 098	25 17 157	37 26 208	35 11 267	41 33 289	48 11 336
	Dubhe	Denebola	•SPICA	ACRUX	•CANOPUS	SIRIUS	•POLLUX
135	14 17 014	41 33 060	25 09 098	25 41 157	36 58 209	56 25 255	47 46 335
136	14 31 014	42 24 059	26 07 098	26 04 157	36 30 209	55 28 255	47 21 334
137	14 45 014	43 15 059	27 06 097	26 27 157	36 01 210	54 31 255	46 54 333
138	14 59 013	44 05 058	28 05 097	26 49 158	35 32 210	53 33 255	46 26 331
139	15 12 013	44 55 057	29 03 097	27 12 158	35 02 210	52 36 256	45 58 330
140	15 25 012	45 45 057	30 02 097	27 34 158	34 32 211	51 39 256	45 28 329
141	15 37 012	46 34 056	31 00 097	27 55 159	34 01 211	50 42 256	44 57 328
142	15 49 011	47 23 055	31 59 097	28 17 159	33 31 212	49 44 256	44 26 327
143	16 01 011	48 11 054	32 58 097	28 38 159	32 59 212	48 47 256	43 54 326
144	16 11 010	48 59 054	33 56 097	28 59 160	32 28 212	47 50 256	43 20 325
145	16 22 010	49 46 053	34 55 097	29 19 160	31 56 213	46 52 256	42 46 324
146	16 32 010	50 33 052	35 54 097	29 40 160	31 24 213	45 55 256	42 12 324
147	16 42 009	51 19 051	36 53 096	29 59 161	30 52 213	44 58 256	41 36 323
148	16 51 009	52 04 050	37 51 096	30 19 161	30 19 214	44 00 256	41 00 322
149	16 59 008	52 49 049	38 50 096	30 38 161	29 46 214	43 03 256	40 23 321
	Dubhe	ARCTURUS	•SPICA	ACRUX	•CANOPUS	SIRIUS	•POLLUX
150	17 07 008	20 44 065	39 49 096	30 57 162	29 13 214	42 05 256	39 46 320
151	17 15 007	21 37 065	40 47 096	31 15 162	28 40 215	41 08 257	39 08 319
152	17 22 007	22 31 064	41 46 096	31 33 162	28 06 215	40 10 257	38 29 319
153	17 29 006	23 24 064	42 45 096	31 51 163	27 33 215	39 13 257	37 49 318
154	17 35 006	24 17 063	43 44 096	32 08 163	26 59 215	38 15 257	37 10 317
155	17 41 005	25 09 063	44 43 096	32 25 164	26 24 215	37 18 257	36 29 316
156	17 46 005	26 02 063	45 41 096	32 41 164	25 50 216	36 20 257	35 48 316
157	17 51 004	26 54 062	46 40 096	32 57 165	25 15 216	35 23 257	35 07 315
158	17 55 004	27 47 062	47 39 096	33 12 165	24 41 216	34 25 257	34 25 314
159	17 59 003	28 39 061	48 38 095	33 27 165	24 06 216	33 28 257	33 42 314
160	18 02 003	29 30 061	49 37 095	33 42 166	23 31 216	32 31 256	32 59 313
161	18 04 002	30 22 061	50 35 095	33 56 166	22 55 217	31 33 256	32 16 313
162	18 07 002	31 13 060	51 34 095	34 10 167	22 20 217	30 36 256	31 32 312
163	18 08 001	32 04 060	52 33 095	34 23 167	21 45 217	29 38 256	30 48 311
164	18 09 001	32 55 059	53 32 095	34 36 168	21 09 217	28 41 256	30 04 311
	Dubhe	•ARCTURUS	SPICA	•ACRUX	Suhail	SIRIUS	•POLLUX
165	18 10 000	33 46 059	54 31 095	34 48 168	48 38 211	27 43 256	29 19 310
166	18 10 000	34 36 058	55 30 095	35 00 169	48 07 212	26 46 256	28 34 310
167	18 10 359	35 26 058	56 29 095	35 11 169	47 35 213	25 49 256	27 48 309
168	18 09 359	36 16 057	57 27 095	35 21 170	47 03 213	24 51 256	27 02 309
169	18 07 358	37 05 056	58 26 095	35 31 170	46 30 214	23 54 256	26 16 308
170	18 05 358	37 54 056	59 25 095	35 41 171	45 57 215	22 57 256	25 29 308
171	18 03 357	38 43 055	60 24 095	35 50 171	45 23 216	21 59 256	24 42 307
172	18 00 357	39 31 055	61 23 095	35 59 172	44 48 216	21 02 256	23 55 307
173	17 56 356	40 19 054	62 22 095	36 07 172	44 13 217	20 05 256	23 08 306
174	17 52 356	41 07 053	63 21 095	36 14 173	43 37 217	19 07 256	22 20 306
175	17 48 355	41 54 053	64 20 095	36 21 174	43 01 218	18 10 256	21 33 306
176	17 43 355	42 41 052	65 18 095	36 27 174	42 25 218	17 13 255	20 44 305
177	17 38 354	43 27 051	66 17 095	36 33 175	41 48 219	16 16 255	19 56 305
178	17 32 354	44 13 050	67 16 095	36 38 175	41 11 219	15 19 255	19 07 305
179	17 25 353	44 58 049	68 15 095	36 43 176	40 33 220	14 21 255	18 19 304

Table 10. A page from AP3270 Sight Reduction Tables for Air Navigation Volume I.

6 Sun sights

For many yacht navigators Sun sights form the guts of the whole business. They are taken during the forenoon or afternoon; a forenoon sight produces a position line which, when 'run up' along the course line to the noon latitude, will give a running fix to supply a noon position. Similarly, the noon latitude can be advanced to the PL produced by the afternoon sight to give a running fix later in the day. The afternoon PL can also be transferred back to the noon latitude to check the noon position.

This system is called 'Sun-run-Sun' and can be operated effectively in quite poor weather conditions. A good navigator needs only a glimpse of the Sun to achieve an altitude. The limitations of the method are obvious. We all know the inaccuracies of the running fix from our efforts along the coast. Also, you can only have one noon fix per day. While it is possible to transfer one Sun PL up to another taken quite soon afterwards, the small change in their angles means that the resulting 'cut' of the PLs

will be very poor. In general, a forenoon sight should be taken not less than one and a half hours before noon. How much earlier you take it will be a trade-off. The earlier the better for the cut of the position lines, but this will mean a longer run-up for the transferred position line to the noon latitude. The longer the run, the bigger the error, particularly if the current is in doubt. Despite these reservations, a good Sun sight is a very useful thing to have, particularly when the stars and planets are obscured by cloud, or you expect a landfall before dusk.

In Chapter 5 we found that what was needed to plot a sight, any sight, was an *assumed position*, an *azimuth* and an *intercept*.

Sight reduction

You will almost certainly be reducing your sights using sight reduction tables. These come in either a marine form running to several volumes, or a condensed version officially for aviators which gets the number of books down

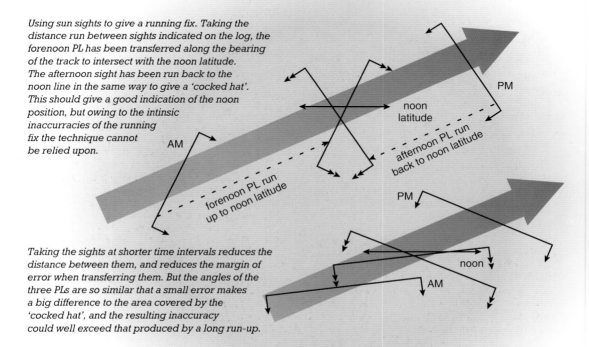

Using sun sights to give a running fix. Taking the distance run between sights indicated on the log, the forenoon PL has been transferred along the bearing of the track to intersect with the noon latitude. The afternoon sight has been run back to the noon line in the same way to give a 'cocked hat'. This should give a good indication of the noon position, but owing to the intinsic inaccurracies of the running fix the technique cannot be relied upon.

AM

noon latitude

PM

forenoon PL run up to noon latitude

afternoon PL run back to noon latitude

PM

noon

AM

Taking the sights at shorter time intervals reduces the distance between them, and reduces the margin of error when transferring them. But the angles of the three PLs are so similar that a small error makes a big difference to the area covered by the 'cocked hat', and the resulting inaccuracy could well exceed that produced by a long run-up.

to three. The latter are more economical to buy and take up less room on board. They are nominally slightly less accurate than the marine equivalent, but since this results from the air tables rounding up or down for decimals of minutes of declination, it is a simple matter to make up this deficiency by interpolation if it really worries you. The business of sight reduction is dealt with in this book on the basis of the *Sight Reduction Tables for Air Navigation* (AP 3270 in the UK, or Pub. No.249 in the US). Volume 1 deals with stars, while volumes 2 and 3 handle all celestial bodies with a declination of less than 30°. This encompasses everything in the solar system: the Moon, the planets and, needless to say, the Sun itself.

Calculators

It is possible to buy pre-programmed navigation calculators loaded with almanac information as well as complete sight reduction data. These remarkable pieces of kit will reduce your sights and give azimuth and intercept from a DR or an assumed position. The advantages are obvious, but it is recommended that before relying upon them as a primary tool, the following simple methods based on tables are mastered. In any case, it would be foolish to go to sea without an almanac and a set of sight reduction tables, lest all else should fail.

THE ASSUMED POSITION

Assumed latitude

You can rarely reduce a sight using your DR latitude because the sight reduction tables will only give you altitudes and azimuths from positions whose latitudes are *whole numbers*. The first thing to do then, is shift your DR latitude to the nearest whole degree. This is called the *assumed latitude*.

Assumed longitude

Next, doctor your DR longitude so that the LHA of the Sun for the time of your sight turns out to be a whole number as well. The reason for this is that, once again, the tables will tolerate no fractions of degrees of LHA.

Now work out the GHA for the Sun at the time of your sight and then, if in west longitude, juggle your DR so that the minutes and decimals are the same as those of the Sun's GHA. When you subtract the longitude from the GHA they will disappear. (See page 11: Local Hour Angle.)

In east longitude, you adjust the minutes of longitude so that when added to the minutes and seconds of the Sun's GHA they add up to a whole number. It's as simple as that.

Example 1: DR longitude 17° 46′W

Sun's GHA at 04h 12m 07s	242°	57′	.3
- Assumed longitude west	17°	57′	.3
LHA	225°		

Example 2: DR longitude 27° 49′E

Sun's GHA at 04h 12m 07s	242°	57′	.3
+ Assumed longitude east	28°	02′	.7
LHA	271°		

AZIMUTH AND INTERCEPT

A working page from Volume 3 of AP 3270 will be found on page 37. Notice that the top right-hand corner gives the latitude 49°. There is a different set of pages for each latitude. Which page of the set you choose is decided by the top central legend, which in this case reads 'Declin-ation (15°-29°) SAME name as latitude'. This means that to choose the right page you need to know the declination of the Sun (obtained from *The Nautical Almanac*) as well as your assumed latitude.

On the extreme left and right of the page are columns showing LHA. Choose the value your assumed position has given and move across into the page until you reach the correct column for your declination (shown in the boxes at top and bottom of the page). You will see that three figures are given, labelled 'Hc', 'd' and 'Z'.

Azimuth

'Z' is the figure from which you find the Sun's azimuth (Zn). The formula for doing this is to be found at the top and bottom left-hand corners of the page - north latitudes at the top, and south latitudes at the bottom, as follows:

N.Lat	LHA greater than 180°...	Zn=Z
	LHA less than 180°...	Zn=360 - Z
S.Lat	LHA greater than 180°...	Zn=180 - Z
	LHA less than 180°...	Zn=180 + Z

Azimuths are, of course, always expressed in degrees True.

Calculated altitude

'Hc' is the calculated altitude for the *whole degree* of declination. To adjust this for minutes of declination take the figure given under 'd'. Using this figure you enter the 'bookmark' table 5 (see page 38). With 'd' as one argument and 'minutes of declination' as the other, extract the value you require and use it to adjust the main figure for Hc. Notice that 'd' is labelled + or – in the main tables. You now have a calculated altitude.

Example

What is the calculated altitude and azimuth for a body whose declination at the time of the sight was 24° 19', whose local hour angle is 315° and which was observed from an assumed latitude of 49°N?

Find the LHA (on the right-hand side of the table) and move across to the column marked 24°. This gives you the following:

Hc 46 57   d + 44   Z 109

Since you are in northern latitudes and the LHA is greater than 180°, Zn=Z. So the azimuth (Zn) is 109°.

As for the calculated altitude, you need to go to the 'bookmark' (page 35). Find 44 in the 'd' column down the side, and move across to the figure in the column beneath the figure 19 (remember that the declination is 24° 19'). This gives you 14, and since the 'd' figure is +44 the resulting increment is + 14.

Hc	46° 57'
d + 44	14'
Hc	47° 11'

You now have an *assumed position* and an *azimuth*. By finding the difference between the calculated altitude above and your observed (corrected sextant) altitude, you have an *intercept* as well.

PRODUCING A SUN SIGHT

1 Put your pro-forma ready on the chart table (see opposite). After you've crossed the Atlantic once, you won't need it any more, but it will help a lot in the early days.
2 Go up on deck, take a sight of the Sun, time it and then read the log. Make sure the time is right because every four seconds can give an error of up to one mile.
3 Fill in 'watch time' in the pro-forma. Correct for GMT.
4 Extract the Sun's GHA and declination for the hour concerned from the daily pages of *The Nautical Almanac*. Enter them in the pro-forma.
5 Work up the actual declination for the minute of the sight, using the 'd' correction if you need to (see page 11). Round any decimals up or down.
6 Turn to the increments pages of the almanac for the minutes and seconds of GHA (see page 32) and enter them in the pro-forma. Work up the Sun's GHA (see page 9).
7 Decide on a suitable assumed longitude and

enter it so as to come up with an LHA for the Sun as a whole number of degrees (see page 41). While you are about it, decide on your assumed latitude and enter it. This will give you your assumed position.
8 Open your sight reduction tables (AP 3270). Check that you have the right page with reference to your assumed latitude, the 'name' of the Sun's declination etc. Extract 'Hc', 'd' and 'Z' and enter them on the pro-forma. Take care to note the sign of 'd'. Is it + or – ?
9 While Ap 3270 is open, check what to do with 'Z' to convert it to 'Zn', and thereby provide you with an azimuth (see page 41). Enter this in the pro-forma.
10 Consult the 'bookmark' Table 5 in AP 3270 to deal with the minutes of declination (see page 41). Enter the answer and then work up the final, corrected, calculated altitude (Hc).
11 Enter your sextant reading in the pro-forma. Enter the index error (if any) and dip, (see page 17) then work up the apparent altitude. Extract the altitude correction from the 'bookmark' of The Nautical Almanac (the left-hand table), enter it and work up the true altitude (Ho).
12 Compare this with Hc; the difference is your intercept (see page 28). Label it towards or away, and you have all you need to plot your sight (see Chapter 5).

USING THE SIGHT

If you take a forenoon sight like this at about 0930 local time and then run it up to your noon latitude by transferring the position line along your course line the appropriate number of miles, you will have a fix at the point where the transferred position line cuts the latitude (see page 40).

You can check this by taking another observation in the afternoon, between 1400 and 1500 local time, and then running the PL back. See what sort of cocked hat you produce and evaluate the result. In good conditions you could expect to achieve an area of probable position two to four miles across. You may do much better - but remember, at best this is only a running fix.

Sorting the good from the bad

The more experienced you are, the easier it is to assess the quality of a particular sight. If you are in doubt about the standard of an important one, and if conditions and time available for navigation permit, take a series of observations (five or seven is customary) and graph the results, time against altitude.

PRO-FORMA FOR SUN SIGHT

Date **1 MAY 1986**

DR 49° 12'N
5° 10' W

Watch time	**09 15 23**			
Correction	**FAST -6**			
GMT	**09h 15m 17s**			

GHA (hrs)	**315° 43'.4**	
+Correction (mins/secs)	**3 49.3**	
GHA	**319 32.7**	
Assumed Long	**5 32.7**	Assumed Lat **49°N**
LHA	**314°**	

Hc	**39 28**	z	**116**	Declination (hrs)	**15 02'N**
d ~~+47~~	**+2**	~~180/360~~		d difference ~~07~~	**+0.2**
Hc	**39° 30'**	Zn	**116**	Declination	**15° 02'.3N**

Hs	**39° 28**
Index Error	**- -**
Dip **8 FEET**	**-02.7**
Apparent Alt	**39 25.3**
Main Correction	**+14.8**
Ho	**39 40.1**
Hc	**39 30**
Intercept	**10.1** TOWARDS/~~AWAY~~

**Use the blank proforma on
page 64 for your own working.**

The good sights should produce a reasonably straight line. Any duffers can be thrown out, and a time and altitude average taken for those which remain. That is the value to use in your workings.

At this point, let me remind you that most difficulties and errors arise from carelessness in looking things up or in reading the sextant. Keep a firm grip on your head. Go one step at a time and every sight will be a winner.

Now try it

1st May 1986. You take a forenoon sight at 09h 15m 23s watch time. The sextant altitude was 39° 28' and the log read 206.4. Your height of eye was estimated to be eight feet, your watch was six seconds fast and your sextant has no index error. Your DR position was 49° 12'N 5° 10'W. At noon the log reads 218.9 and you observe your latitude to be 49° 15.5. You have been steering 085°T and the tide has cancelled itself out. Plot your position line.

You will find the working and the finished plot below. Don't look at it now; use it to check your own efforts. Working through an example like this is the best way to learn, and with a subject like celestial navigation it is probably the *only* way.

This chapter on Sun sights is very important. In many ways it forms the basis for most of the subsequent chapters, so make sure you understand it thoroughly before standing on any further.

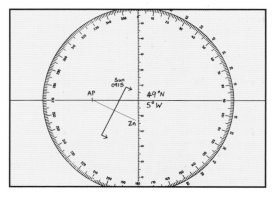

7 The planets

Of the various planets in the solar system, only Venus, Mars, Jupiter and Saturn are useful to the navigator. If they are available for observation they will be clearly visible at twilight, morning or evening. The planets burn so brightly that once you have worked out where one is likely to be, it is extremely easy to identify. The method for reducing your observation to a position line is very similar to that used for the Sun.

TWILIGHT

If you want to measure the altitude of any heavenly body you need a horizon. At night there is generally no horizon and in the daytime you can't see the stars and planets, so the time to observe them is *twilight*.

In practice, the time span of twilight is obvious. In the evening it starts when you see the first planet or star appear and ends when you can no longer discern a horizon. In the morning, it begins as the horizon firms up into a line and ends when the brightest star disappears.

This period, depending on season and latitude, is generally within 20 minutes (plus or minus) of the time of *civil twilight* which is tabulated for various latitudes on the daily pages of *The Nautical Almanac*.

If you are pre-computing the approximate position of a planet, and certainly when you come to work out which star is which (see Chapter 9), you will need to know the time of civil twilight for your rough position.

Don't get bogged down with 'nautical twilight', since it is not relevant to your calculations. Just look up the time of civil twilight (CT) in the almanac, make a mental interpolation for latitude, and you will have it in GMT for the Greenwich Meridian. A quick arc-to-time calculation will adjust this for your own longitude.

Example
May 3rd 1986. What time approximately is civil twilight in the morning at DR 22°N 55°W? See page 31. Interpolating between 20°N and 30°N, civil twilight on the Greenwich Meridian at 22°N is 0504 GMT. Since the Sun is moving

towards the west, twilight will be later in 55° west longitude by 55 x 4 minutes = 220 minutes = 3h 40 minutes. Therefore civil twilight is at 0844 GMT at our position.

PLANET IDENTIFICATION

There is a fine description of the planets and their movements in *The Nautical Almanac* which tells you which planet is likely to be where. You may also find the data in other sources, but the most accurate method for finding a planet is as follows.

Extract the time of civil twilight and then, using a planet pro-forma, enter this time as the time of an observation. Working from this, consult the almanac to find an approximate LHA, assumed latitude and declination for the planet concerned (you can be very rough) and enter the sight reduction tables. These will give you a calculated altitude and an azimuth. Don't bother to correct the calculated altitude for minutes of declination.

At twilight, sight along the azimuth and look up to something like the calculated altitude. The bright star there is your planet.

Once you have a planet well and truly recognised you can, in all probability, use it for the rest of the voyage. They don't change their position very rapidly so you don't have to go through this every day.

It is said that with careful pre-computing you can find Venus in your sextant telescope during the day and so take a sight of it. Bright though it undoubtedly is, I have had no luck with this one. You might like to try it all the same because it could be extremely useful. I'm still working on it myself...

SHOOTING A PLANET OR STAR

Having identified your planet you'll find shooting it is easier than the Sun. There is always a hint of doubt about when the Sun's lower limb is perfectly on the horizon, but a star or planet is just a point source of light. It is either on the horizon or it isn't. Pull it down, give the sextant wrist a quick pendulum

The planets are so much brighter than the stars that they are easy to identify and can be seen when the sky is quite bright. This is Venus rising (time-lapse photography).

twist to ensure you are perpendicular, and note the time.

PLANET SIGHT REDUCTION

A study of the planet pro-forma will show that the system for working out a planet sight is virtually identical to that used for the Sun. There are, however, a few small differences.

The 'v' correction for GHA
This is an extra incremental correction for the GHA of a planet. You will find 'v' alongside 'd' at the bottom of the daily page column for your planet in the almanac. You apply it to GHA in the same way that you apply 'd' for declination. You can look it up at the same time as you check your GHA minutes and seconds increment. Notice that it is not always positive. For Venus, for example, 'v' is sometimes negative - so watch out.

Apparent altitude and parallax
As with the Sun, you have to apply an apparent altitude correction to your sextant altitude after dealing with index error and dip. You will find the correction in the centre of the bookmark page of the almanac. The figure is much smaller for stars and planets than for the Sun. This is because it contains no correction for semi-diameter.

Don't forget that Mars and Venus may have an additional small correction for parallax (see page 18). This can be found alongside the apparent altitude correction on the bookmark page. Apply it below the apparent altitude correction in the sextant corrections on the pro-forma.

Example
May 1st 1986. You are in DR 49°N 35° 30'W and you observe Venus through the sextant telescope at 20h 15m 18s watch time. Your watch is set to GMT, and is 10 seconds slow. Sextant altitude is 33° 13'.6, index error is 2.8' on the arc and you estimate your height of eye to be 12 feet. Plot your position line.

The completed pro-forma and plot are illustrated overleaf - but see if you can do it yourself first.

PRO-FORMA FOR PLANET SIGHT

Date	**1 MAY 1986**	Watch time	20 15 18
Planet	VENUS	Correction	+10
DR	49°N 35° 30' W	GMT	20 15 28

GHA (hrs)	95 19.9		
+Correction (mins/secs)	3 52.0		
v (−0.8)	−0.2		
GHA	99 11.7		
Assumed Long	35 11.7 W	Assumed Lat	49° N
LHA	64°		

Hc	33 19	z	94	Declination (hrs)	22 02.3N	
d (+43)	+2	180/360	360−94	d (0.6+)	+0.2	
Hc	33 21	Zn	266	Declination	22 02.5N	

Hs	33 13.6
Index Error	−2.8
Dip	−3.4
Apparent Alt	33 07.4
Correction	−01.5
Parallax	+00.1
Ho	33 06
Hc	33 21
Intercept	15 AWAY

That is all there is to planet sights. They can be useful on their own, and can often form part of a set of star and planet sights for a good fix at twilight. You can also make them part of a running fix by transferring an afternoon Sun PL up to an evening planet PL, or transferring a morning planet PL up to the forenoon Sun sight.

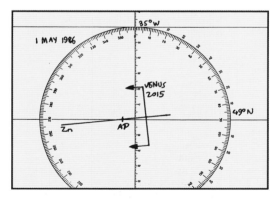

8 The Moon

Traditionally, while the Moon has delighted poets down the ages, it has not been the navigator's favourite body. This is because it requires just a little extra effort to reduce a Moon sight and therefore leaves more room for the careless to come unstuck. 'The Moon is inaccurate', they howl, shaking their fists at it. The Moon is no such thing. All its movements are ordered and they are all tabulated in the almanac. It's up to you, mate, what you make of it.

The wonderful thing about the Moon is that it is often visible at the same time as the Sun and at a reasonable angular distance from it. This gives you the opportunity to take *simultaneous sights* and achieve a real fix, albeit a two-point one.

'Simultaneous' means, in this context, taking two or more sights within such a short time that you do not have to bother about how far you have run between them. If you are doing five knots and you take two sights five minutes apart, your change of position isn't going to make a lot of difference to the results.

Generally the Moon is usefully available for observation a few days before and after half Moon, both waxing and waning, but it also offers itself at other times.

CORRECTIONS IN SIGHT REDUCTION

As a basic proposition, the closer the target to Earth, the more corrections you will have to make when reducing the sight. The Moon, a mere 250,000 miles away, is particularly susceptible. Its GHA varies a lot from the regular, as does the rate of change in declination. Its closeness also makes horizontal parallax a very real factor when correcting apparent altitude.

Upper and lower limb
Unlike the Sun, which usually presents us with a view of its whole disc, the Moon is frequently partially obscured. In many of its phases you have no choice but to shoot the upper limb. Shooting the 'ghostly galleon' can be pleasant, but often you are stuck with the dreaded inverted melon slice. For some reason this is more difficult to observe accurately.

Horizontal parallax corrections are tabulated for both the upper and lower limb. All other corrections assume that you are taking a lower limb observation. This creates no problems, however, because if you shoot the upper limb you simply subtract 30′ from your corrected altitude and that takes care of the matter.

THE MOON SIGHT PRO-FORMA

When you refer to the Moon in the daily pages of the almanac (see page 31) you will see that there are five columns of information. GHA we know about, and 'v' is just the same as for the planets: it is the increment by which the GHA varies from the regular. Because this changes so frequently in the case of the Moon, it warrants a column of its own. Note that the Moon also has its own column in the increment tables for minutes and seconds of time for GHA as well.

Declination is self-explanatory and 'd', the increment correction, is treated like 'v' because of its rapid variations.

The only newcomer is the horizontal parallax (HP) column. You will find a space on the pro-forma for 'HP' in the altitude corrections, because HP (see page 14) represents an error in the observed altitude.

All these values are entered into the pro-forma (see page 49). Note that 'v' is always *added* to the GHA because the Moon rises later each day.

Like all declination increments, 'd' may be added or subtracted. Find out which by inspection of the hours adjacent to the one you are interested in. If the declination is increasing by the hour, then the 'd' value is positive. If it is decreasing, then it is negative.

Everything else is straightforward until you come to the *altitude*.

ALTITUDE CORRECTION TABLES FOR THE MOON

These are to be found at the very back of the almanac. They are easy enough to follow and the system described in the tables leaves no doubt

App. Alt.	0°–4° Corrⁿ	5°–9° Corrⁿ	10°–14° Corrⁿ	15°–19° Corrⁿ	20°–24° Corrⁿ	25°–29° Corrⁿ	30°–34° Corrⁿ	App. Alt.
00	0 33.8	5 58.2	10 62.1	15 62.8	20 62.2	25 60.8	30 58.9	00
10	35.9	58.5	62.2	62.8	62.1	60.8	58.8	10
20	37.8	58.7	62.2	62.8	62.1	60.7	58.8	20
30	39.6	58.9	62.3	62.8	62.1	60.7	58.7	30
40	41.2	59.1	62.3	62.8	62.0	60.6	58.6	40
50	42.6	59.3	62.4	62.7	62.0	60.6	58.5	50
00	1 44.0	6 59.5	11 62.4	16 62.7	21 62.0	26 60.5	31 58.5	00
10	45.2	59.7	62.4	62.7	61.9	60.4	58.4	10
20	46.3	59.9	62.5	62.7	61.9	60.4	58.3	20
30	47.3	60.0	62.5	62.7	61.9	60.3	58.2	30
40	48.3	60.2	62.5	62.7	61.8	60.3	58.2	40
50	49.2	60.3	62.6	62.7	61.8	60.2	58.1	50
00	2 50.0	7 60.5	12 62.6	17 62.7	22 61.7	27 60.1	32 58.0	00
10	50.8	60.6	62.6	62.7	61.7	60.1	57.9	10
20	51.4	60.7	62.6	62.6	61.6	60.0	57.8	20
30	52.1	60.9	62.7	62.6	61.6	59.9	57.8	30
40	52.7	61.0	62.7	62.6	61.5	59.9	57.7	40
50	53.3	61.1	62.7	62.6	61.5	59.8	57.6	50
00	3 53.8	8 61.2	13 62.7	18 62.5	23 61.5	28 59.7	33 57.5	00
10	54.3	61.3	62.7	62.5	61.4	59.7	57.4	10
20	54.8	61.4	62.7	62.5	61.4	59.6	57.4	20
30	55.2	61.5	62.8	62.5	61.3	59.6	57.3	30
40	55.6	61.6	62.8	62.4	61.3	59.5	57.2	40
50	56.0	61.6	62.8	62.4	61.2	59.4	57.1	50
00	4 56.4	9 61.7	14 62.8	19 62.4	24 61.2	29 59.3	34 57.0	00
10	56.7	61.8	62.8	62.3	61.1	59.3	56.9	10
20	57.1	61.9	62.8	62.3	61.1	59.2	56.9	20
30	57.4	61.9	62.8	62.3	61.0	59.1	56.8	30
40	57.7	62.0	62.8	62.2	60.9	59.1	56.7	40
50	57.9	62.1	62.8	62.2	60.9	59.0	56.6	50

H.P.	L	U	L	U	L	U	L	U	L	U	L	U	L	U	H.P.
54.0	0.3	0.9	0.3	0.9	0.4	1.0	0.5	1.1	0.6	1.2	0.7	1.3	0.9	1.5	54.0
54.3	0.7	1.1	0.7	1.2	0.7	1.2	0.8	1.3	0.9	1.4	1.1	1.5	1.2	1.7	54.3
54.6	1.1	1.4	1.1	1.4	1.1	1.4	1.2	1.5	1.3	1.6	1.4	1.7	1.5	1.8	54.6
54.9	1.4	1.6	1.5	1.6	1.5	1.6	1.6	1.7	1.6	1.8	1.8	1.9	1.9	2.0	54.9
55.2	1.8	1.8	1.8	1.8	1.9	1.9	1.9	1.9	2.0	2.0	2.1	2.1	2.2	2.2	55.2
55.5	2.2	2.0	2.2	2.0	2.3	2.1	2.3	2.1	2.4	2.2	2.4	2.3	2.5	2.4	55.5
55.8	2.6	2.2	2.6	2.2	2.6	2.3	2.7	2.3	2.7	2.4	2.8	2.4	2.9	2.5	55.8
56.1	3.0	2.4	3.0	2.5	3.0	2.5	3.0	2.5	3.1	2.6	3.1	2.6	3.2	2.7	56.1
56.4	3.4	2.7	3.4	2.7	3.4	2.7	3.4	2.7	3.4	2.8	3.5	2.8	3.5	2.9	56.4
56.7	3.7	2.9	3.7	2.9	3.8	2.9	3.8	2.9	3.8	3.0	3.8	3.0	3.9	3.0	56.7
57.0	4.1	3.1	4.1	3.1	4.1	3.1	4.1	3.1	4.2	3.1	4.2	3.2	4.2	3.2	57.0
57.3	4.5	3.3	4.5	3.3	4.5	3.3	4.5	3.3	4.5	3.3	4.5	3.4	4.6	3.4	57.3
57.6	4.9	3.5	4.9	3.5	4.9	3.5	4.9	3.5	4.9	3.5	4.9	3.5	4.9	3.6	57.6
57.9	5.3	3.8	5.3	3.8	5.2	3.8	5.2	3.7	5.2	3.7	5.2	3.7	5.2	3.7	57.9
58.2	5.6	4.0	5.6	4.0	5.6	4.0	5.6	4.0	5.6	3.9	5.6	3.9	5.6	3.9	58.2
58.5	6.0	4.2	6.0	4.2	6.0	4.2	6.0	4.2	6.0	4.1	5.9	4.1	5.9	4.1	58.5
58.8	6.4	4.4	6.4	4.4	6.4	4.4	6.3	4.4	6.3	4.3	6.3	4.3	6.2	4.2	58.8
59.1	6.8	4.6	6.8	4.6	6.7	4.6	6.7	4.6	6.7	4.5	6.6	4.5	6.6	4.4	59.1
59.4	7.2	4.8	7.1	4.8	7.1	4.8	7.1	4.8	7.0	4.7	7.0	4.7	6.9	4.6	59.4
59.7	7.5	5.1	7.5	5.0	7.5	5.0	7.5	5.0	7.4	4.9	7.3	4.8	7.2	4.7	59.7
60.0	7.9	5.3	7.9	5.3	7.9	5.2	7.8	5.2	7.8	5.1	7.7	5.0	7.6	4.9	60.0
60.3	8.3	5.5	8.3	5.5	8.2	5.4	8.2	5.4	8.1	5.3	8.0	5.2	7.9	5.1	60.3
60.6	8.7	5.7	8.7	5.7	8.6	5.7	8.6	5.6	8.5	5.5	8.4	5.4	8.2	5.3	60.6
60.9	9.1	5.9	9.0	5.9	9.0	5.9	8.9	5.8	8.8	5.7	8.7	5.6	8.6	5.4	60.9
61.2	9.5	6.2	9.4	6.1	9.4	6.1	9.3	6.0	9.2	5.9	9.1	5.8	8.9	5.6	61.2
61.5	9.8	6.4	9.8	6.3	9.7	6.3	9.7	6.2	9.5	6.1	9.4	5.9	9.2	5.8	61.5

One of the altitude correction tables for the Moon from the end of the Nautical Almanac.

about how this should be done. So 'when all else fails, read the instructions'. They even give you a 'dip' table on the same page so that you don't have to scrabble through the book looking for the one you use for everything else.

Correct your sextant altitude for index error and dip just as you would for any other sight. This gives you your apparent altitude.

There are now two corrections to apply. The *first correction* is found in the upper section of the altitude correction tables for the Moon. It is straightforward enough, but is set out in a rather unusual manner. The only argument for entry into the table is apparent altitude. Here are two examples to help you familiarise yourself with it.

Example 1

Your apparent altitude is 12° 20′. What is the first correction?
Find 12° (one of the bold figures in the body of the table), then go down the adjacent column until you find the correction figure opposite 20′ in the **App Alt** column. The answer is 62.6′

Example 2

Your apparent altitude is 34° 37′. What is the first correction?
The answer is 56.7′.

The *second correction* will refer to horizontal parallax (HP) which you extract from the fifth 'Moon' column of the daily page in the almanac and note on your pro-forma. The Moon altitude correction table is entered with HP as your argument (side columns). Move across the table until you are in the column from which you took the first correction for apparent altitude. 'L' and 'U' refer to the upper and lower limb and you can choose accordingly.

Example 3

What are corrections 1 and 2 for an apparent altitude of 25° 42′ and an HP figure of 56.4? The sight was of the Moon's lower limb.
Correction 1 is 60.6.
Correction 2 is 3.5, obtained by dropping straight down the column from correction 1 and selecting the sub-column headed L'.

Both corrections are added to the apparent altitude and when applied give the true altitude (Ho) for the Moon's *lower* limb. If you observed the *upper* limb, you'll have to subtract 30′ from the result, as in the third

PRO-FORMA FOR MOON SIGHT

Date **1 MAY 1986**	Watch time **10 1409**
	Correction
DR: 41°S 25° 38'E	GMT **10 1409**

GHA (hrs)	**50° 45.9**		
+ Correction (mins/secs)	**3 22.6**		
+ v **(09.2)**	**2.2**		
GHA	**54 10.7**		
Assumed Long	**25 49.3E**	Assumed Lat	**41°S**
LHA	**80°**		

Hc	**20 57**	z	**80**	Declination (hrs)	**21 27.8 S**
+36	**15**	180/360	**+180**	d **-(10.8)**	**-2.6**
Hc	**21 12**	Zn	**260**	Declination	**21 25.2 S**

Hs	**20 48.2**
Index Error	**-1 ON**
Dip	**-3.4**
Apparent Alt	**20 43.8**
+ 1st correction	**62.0**
+ 2nd correction	**3.7**
Ho Lower Limb	**21 49.5**
3rd Correction	**-0 30.0**
Ho Upper Limb	**21 19.5**
Hc	**21 12**
INTERCEPT	**7.5** TOWARDS/~~AWAY~~

Hp **57.8**

correction on the pro-forma. This compensates for the Moon's diameter.

You now have all the information you need to take a Moon sight.

Example 4

May 1st, 1986. You are in DR 41° S 25° 38'E and are able to observe the Moon's upper limb. The time is 10h 14m 09s GMT (you have just adjusted your watch) and the sextant altitude was 20° 48.2. Index error is 1' on the arc and your height of eye is about 12 feet. Plot your position line. The worked pro-forma and plot are shown here, but as before, see if you can figure out the answer yourself.

If you use your pro-forma as a guide and work through it step by step, Moon sight reduction should not prove a problem. If, however, you are struggling to cope with the Moon's eccentricities, leave it alone for a while and

go on to the stars. These are the easiest of the lot to reduce and, as you'll see, simple to identify. You will find that they are of immense importance to your navigation.

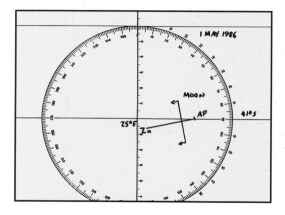

9 The stars

Most people who dabble in celestial navigation are under the mistaken impression that star sights are a problem. This misconception arises from two great fallacies:

1 It is difficult to identify the star you want because it is twilight and the constellations are invisible, and you would be involved in an unacceptable amount of rote learning to memorise all the names.

2 Working out star sights is complicated and plotting is a nightmare.

These objections are complete nonsense, and here's why:

1 You don't personally have to identify the star you require because Volume 1 of AP 3270 does it for you. The arithmetic needed to extract the information can be readily handled by a ten-year-old.

Like many of us, you may choose to identify the stars by name for your own satisfaction. If the night is bright and it's your watch, what better way can there be of keeping awake to your place in the universe than kitting yourself up with a well-laced coffee and a star map, and watching the stars in their courses. The names are as beautiful as the starts themselves: Aldebaran, Sirius, Procyon and the rest. While you are out there, treat yourself to a look into the Pleiades or the nebula in the Sword of Orion with your ship's binoculars. As the sky leaps into 3-D, it is like peering down the throat of infinity. However, if all this fails to turn you on, stick with the simple arithmetic. It won't let you down.

2 Working out sights and plotting them is like every other job - building a boat, climbing a mountain, or even installing central heating. If you squint up the hill from the beginning to the end result, it is a daunting prospect, but if you take the task as a series of small stages leading towards completion, you will overcome the psychological barrier with ease. Indeed, if you reconsider the apparently complicated star pro-forma you'll realise that it is actually the simplest of all.

Just as a guide, a competent navigator working with a mate to note the times of the observations can shoot seven stars in about fifteen minutes on a good evening. It will then take another half hour or so to reduce and plot them. For less than an hour's pleasant work you can produce a fix which could well be good to a mile or less anywhere on the Earth, using bodies whose distance away from us shivers the brain on its mountings.

Brightness of stars (magnitude)

There are over 4,000 stars visible from Earth, but the vast majority are of no benefit to the navigator. There are 57 which are readily identified and bright enough to be used. These 57 are indexed in the almanac and also on the back of the bookmark page. This gives the name of each star, its magnitude, its SHA (Sidereal Hour Angle), of which more shortly, and its approximate declination.

The magnitude of a star is its brightness. The *higher* the number, the *dimmer* the star. Capella at 0.2 is much brighter than Menkar at 2.8. Sirius is so bright it is off the scale and has the negative value of −1.6. The bigger the negative number, the brighter the star.

No.	Name	Mag.	S.H.A.	Dec.
1	*Alpheratz*	2·2	358°	N. 29°
2	*Ankaa*	2·4	354	S. 42
3	*Schedar*	2·5	350	N. 56
4	*Diphda*	2·2	349	S. 18
5	*Achernar*	0·6	336	S. 57
6	*Hamal*	2·2	328	N. 23
7	*Acamar*	3·1	316	S. 40
8	*Menkar*	2·8	315	N. 4
9	*Mirfak*	1·9	309	N. 50
10	*Aldebaran*	1·1	291	N. 16
11	*Rigel*	0·3	282	S. 8
12	*Capella*	0·2	281	N. 46
13	*Bellatrix*	1·7	279	N. 6
14	*Elnath*	1·8	279	N. 29
15	*Alnilam*	1·8	276	S. 1
16	*Betelgeuse*	Var.*	271	N. 7
17	*Canopus*	−0·9	264	S. 53
18	*Sirius*	−1·6	259	S. 17

Part of the index of 57 selected stars.

It is worth noting here that the magnitude of the planets varies and is tabulated in the daily pages of the almanac alongside each planet's name in the top box of the 'planet columns'.

FIRST POINT OF ARIES AND SIDEREAL HOUR ANGLE (SHA)

Because there are so many stars it would be impractical and expensive to tabulate the movements of every one for each day of the year.

Owing to the effectively infinite distance between us and the stars, their positions relative to one another on the celestial sphere do not vary significantly. The declinations of the stars remain the same throughout the year as the Earth moves round its microscopic orbit, but as it turns beneath them once a day, their GHAs advance with a marvellous regularity. Since the stars are a fixed angular distance apart, their GHAs all proceed at the same rate. So if the movement of just one is tabulated and the angles from this to all the others are known, it is a simple matter to calculate the GHA of any star at a given time.

The point on the celestial sphere from which all the other GHAs are calculated is called the *First Point of Aries* and given the symbol of the ram ♈.

The east-west angle between Aries and the position of a given star is known as the *Sidereal Hour Angle* (SHA) of the star; in other words, the

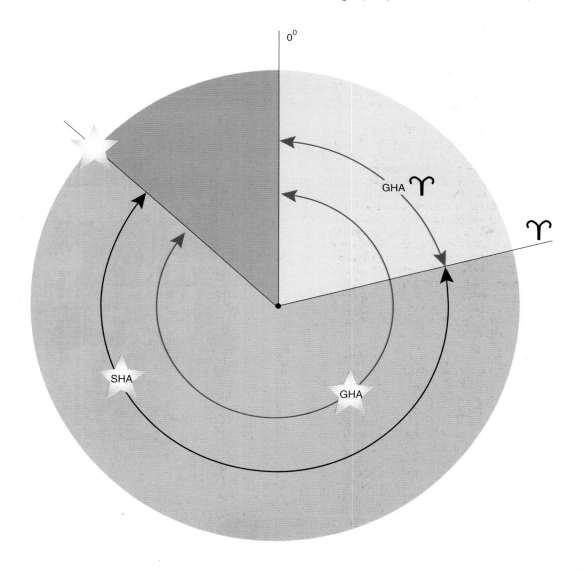

star's SHA is its angular distance to the west of Aries. For example, the GHA of Altair = GHA ♈ + SHA Altair.

If the resulting GHA turns out to be greater than 360°, you should subtract 360 from it to arrive at a workable figure.

If you need to know the exact SHA and declination of a star you will find them tabulated in the daily pages of the almanac, at the right-hand side of the stars and planets half of the double-page daily spread (page 30). They are also set out on the bookmark (page 50), but here they are rounded to the nearest whole number for quick reference.

Example

What is the celestial position (GHA and dec.) of Diphda on May 1st 1986 at 18h 14m 26s?

GHA Aries 18h	129° 22′	.0
+ Increment (page 32)	3° 37′	.1
GHA Aries	132° 59′	.1
+ SHA Diphda	349° 16′	.8
GHA Diphda	482° 15′	.9
— 360	360°	
GHA Diphda	122° 15′	.9

Declination S18°03'.8 (from almanac star tables).

REDUCING A SINGLE STARSIGHT

If the declination of a star is less than 30° then it can be reduced like the Sun or a planet using Volumes 2 or 3 of AP 3270. Work out the GHA of the star from the GHA of Aries and the star's SHA and then proceed. There will be no incremental changes in declination since this is virtually constant.

It is actually quite rare to reduce a starsight like this because of the potential problems of identifying stars and because there is an easier way by using the planned system described below.

Volume 1 of AP 3270 - 'Selected Stars'

When you get hold of a copy of this wonderful book you will see that on the front cover beneath the title it bears the legend, 'Epoch 2000.0'. This edition covers five years either side of 2000. Volumes 2 and 3 go on for as long as you can hold the pages together.

The illustration on page 39 is is a reproduction of a working page from AP 3270 Volume 1. Notice the assumed latitude at the top of the page - this time named north or south (in this case south). The argument for entry is LHA of Aries.

Reading across for a given LHA there are seven stars listed, all with their calculated altitude (Hc) and azimuth (Zn), arrayed in ascending order of azimuth. These are the actual values for this LHA. *No further calculation is required.*

The stars whose names are in capital letters are the brightest, and those marked with the symbol ◆ will, when plotted, give the best 'cut' for a fix.

PLANNING A STARSIGHT SESSION

Given a clear twilight in decent weather there is no reason why, with practice, you should not be able to shoot all seven of the stars recommended for your location in Volume 1. The seven chosen are selected for their probable visibility and their viability as sources of good position lines.

Prepare for them all, then. Even if you don't catch the lot because of cloud, weather or plain incompetence, you should get enough for a fix. But, to be in with a chance of any, you need to know where to find them. Here is the big secret...

1 Determine the time of civil twilight for your DR position (see page 44).
2 Work out the LHA of Aries for this time and location. As always, it needs to be a whole number to enter the tables, so choose an assumed longitude accordingly. You can use the top of the starsight pro-forma for this.
3 Open Volume 1 at the page for your latitude and look up the LHA you have calculated. Those are your stars, together with their altitudes and azimuths for your assumed position. For purposes of finding the stars these values will be as effective as the real values from your actual position.
4 You will probably be able to start observing the brighter stars before the official time of civil twilight. In order to do this you simply go back one degree of LHA for four minutes of time. I generally make a note like this, going forward from civil twilight as well to give myself an extra chance at that end.

Time		LHA
1828		132
1832		133
1836		134
1840	——Civil Twilight——	135
1844		136
1848		137
1852		138

5 Have Volume 1 open on the chart table and your note of LHAs and times (see above) beside it. Give the deck watch to your mate and put your pro-forma on the table as well. No doubt you'll improvise if you have only a small chart table.

6 The moment conditions allow (just before the first star comes out in the evening, or as soon as the eastern horizon firms up in the morning) decide on your first star. It is generally more useful to begin with the stars to the east of you and end with those to the west. The eastern horizon sharpens up first in the morning, and in the evening the western horizon stays visible longest. If there is a lot of cloud about, however, common sense must prevail. Grab what you can when you can.

7 Look up the star's altitude for the *current LHA of Aries* and set your sextant to this figure. Then hang your handbearing compass round your neck and nip up on deck. Use the compass to look down the azimuth of the star (don't forget to allow for magnetic variation: azimuths are in degrees True) and 'fix' the direction with a cloud, or star, or ship, or something. If there is nothing, you'll just have to concentrate harder. Then look towards the horizon in that direction through your preset sextant.

8 If all is well the star will appear somewhere in your field of view. Rack it up or down to the horizon and call 'NOW', at which point your mate marks the exact time. You then go back to the chart table and note the time, the sextant angle and the name of the star in your pro-forma. Read your sextant *carefully*, because there's no going back. Once this is done, you can extract the data on the next star and do it again.

You'll be amazed at how well this works. It may be necessary to 'sweep the horizon' to find the star, but usually they appear without much trouble. Pick bright stars to start with. Some of the feeble ones can be a bit demoralising and may need to be abandoned altogether.

If you can't find a particular star, carry on to the next. You have only a short time to shoot the lot and there is none to waste. If you go for seven, you may not get them all but you should have enough for a satisfactory fix. And if there is a nice, fat planet sidling around the sky, pull it down too for good measure. You may not bother to reduce it, but it could be a useful ace if there is ambiguity in your plot. Planets are always a bonus because they are visible when the sky is too bright to see the stars. For this reason you needn't waste any 'star time' shooting them.

Nab them late in the morning, or early in the evening.

DISTANCE RUN BETWEEN STARSIGHTS

We have seen that the great benefit of a set of 'simultaneous' starsights is that the element of a 'run' between sights is removed and the resulting fix can be far more accurate in consequence. Unfortunately, if your boat is sailing at six knots and it takes you 25 minutes to shoot all your stars, she will have travelled two and a half miles through the water between the first and the last sight.

There are two things you can do about this. If you are in no hurry, the best option is to heave to while you make your observations. This will not only stop your boat, it will also considerably reduce her motion and make your job quicker and easier. If you are cursed with a vessel that won't heave to happily, or if you don't want to stop, you should note the log reading at the beginning, the middle and the end of your set of sights. I generally run the early ones up to the middle sight and the last ones back, so that the time of the actual fix is around the centre of the span of your observations. By reference to the various times and your approximate heading, you can make the necessary adjustments to the position lines in your head with an adequate degree of accuracy. There is no need to cover your plot with a network of confusing spider lines.

MULTIPLE STARSIGHT REDUCTION

If you look at the pro-forma for starsight reduction you'll see that it is in two sections. The first half helps you work out the LHA of Aries, so as to be able to pre-compute which stars to observe (see page 51). To use this part of the form you enter the GHA of Aries for the GMT of civil twilight at your position in the box for GHA, followed by its increments of minutes (seconds don't matter here), and carry on from there.

Whilst taking your sights you will have filled in the names of the stars observed, the exact time of each observation and the sextant altitudes. As you complete the other sections you will find that several of them have the same entry 'across the board'; for example, the 'watch time' correction. The GHA of Aries will be the same if all the observations fall in the same hour, but note that the increments for minutes will vary from sight to sight. So will your assumed longitude because, as with all the other forms for sight reduction, you are going for a whole number of degrees for each LHA of Aries.

Index error can be filled in right across, but watch out for dip. On my boat I have to move around quite a bit to shoot all seven stars. Some I can get from the comfort of the wheel box aft, (height of eye eight feet); for others I have to stand on the bow, (height of eye 13 feet); and it

is not unknown for me to be seen lying in the lee scuppers with my sextant on a calm evening looking under the sails with my height of eye down to four feet at the most.

The corrections to apparent altitude are extracted from the centre column of the bookmark of the almanac and the calculated altitude (Hc) and the azimuth come, of course, from Volume 1 of AP 3270. Your assumed

---

STARSIGHT PRO-FORMA

Date: 1 MAY 1986   Time of CT: 0855 GMT

DR: 10°S 139°E   GHA ♈   338° 57.4
                                     Increment (mins)   13   47.3

Assumed Lat: 10°S   GHA ♈   352   44.7
                                     Ass. Long.   138   15.3

                                     LHA ♈   491 = 131 (-360)

STAR	REGULUS	SPICA	ACRUX	CANOPUS	RIGEL	BETELGEUSE	POLLUX
WATCH TIME CORRECTION	08 54 16 +1	08 56 10 +1	08 46 14 +1	08 50 11 +1	08 52 35 +1	09 00 01 +1	09 06 27 +1
GMT	08 54 17	08 56 11	08 46 15	08 50 12	08 52 36	09 00 02	09 06 28
GHA ♈ INCREMENT	338 57.4 13 36.2	338 57.4 14 05.1	338 57.4 11 35.6	338 57.4 12 35.1	338 57.4 13 11.2	353 59.9 0 00.5	353 59.9 1 37.3
GHA ♈ ASS. LONG.	352 33.6 138 26.4	353 02.5 138 57.5	350 33.0 139 27.0	351 32.5 139 27.5	352 08.6 138 51.4	354 00.4 138 59.6	355 38.2 139 21.8
LHA ♈	491 131	492 132	490 130	491 131	491 131	493 133	495 135
Hs INDEX ERROR DIP	60 13.6 (8') -2.7	22 39.5 (8') -2.7	23 53.9 (12') -3.4	39 05.9 (8') -2.7	37 47.8 (12') -3.4	42 11.5 (8') -2.7	47 04.6 (8') -2.7
APP. ALT. CORRECTION	60 10.9 -0.6	22 36.8 -2.3	23 50.5 -2.2	39 03.2 -1.2	37 44.4 -1.1	42 08.8 -1.1	47 01.9 -0.9
Ho Hc	60 10.3 59 43	22 34.5 22 13	23 48.3 23 41	39 02.0 38 48	37 43.2 38 08	42 07.7 42 28	47 01 47 46
INTERCEPT	27.3 T	21.5 T	7.3 T	14 T	24.8 A	20.3 A	45 A
Zn	044	098	156	207	267	290	335

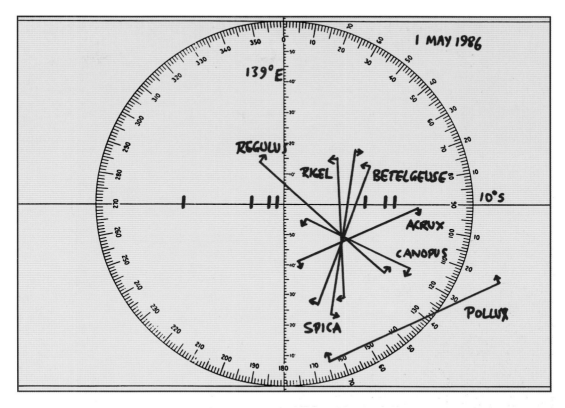

latitude will be the same for all the sights.

Here, then, is a worked example of a set of starsights.

Example

It is 1st May 1986. Your DR position is 10°S 139°E and evening twilight is approaching. What will be the time of civil twilight expressed in GMT at your position? Which stars will you go for? Your sextant has no index error.

From the daily pages of the almanac (see page 31) you'll see that civil twilight in 10°S is at 1811 on the Greenwich meridian.

139° = 9h 16 minutes and because civil twilight, like any other celestial event, will be earlier in east longitude, the GMT of civil twilight in 139°E will be 1811 — 916 = 0855 GMT.

You will not find the minutes and seconds for all the sights on the increments table given on page 16. Space forbids, I fear, so you'll have to take my word for it that the GHA increments are correct.

Don't forget that if you are in doubt as to whether to add or subtract the 9h 16 minutes, a quick look at your navigation clock will show

you the answer. You'll probably be doing the sum in mid-afternoon when the navigation clock shows about 0600 GMT and you know it's about three hours till twilight...

Once you've calculated the GMT time of civil twilight, enter it into the boxes on the upper part of the pro-forma and work out the LHA of Aries at your position for that time.

When you have the LHA you can enter Volume 1 of AP 3270. The illustration on page 39 shows a page for latitude 10°S. You can see the stars available and the Hc and Zn of each for the LHA you've worked out and for several others 'either side' of it.

The lower part of the pro-forma is filled out for the sights and times as they were actually taken. The plot illustrated shows the resulting position lines. Notice that there are no azimuths on the plot. With seven position lines to draw on the chart, marking in seven azimuths as well would just confuse the issue and make the plot unreadable. I generally lay my protractor up the direction of the azimuth from the AP, make a mark at the point where the intercept crosses it ('towards' or 'away', of course) and then construct the PL from that point by adding 90° to the direction of the azimuth.

Five of the position lines form a lovely fix, but you'll notice that Acrux is slightly outside, while Pollux is a long way adrift. In a situation like this it would be a safe assumption that what you thought was Pollux was something else (Castor, perhaps - this is not uncommon by any means). I would suggest discarding that one.

Acrux is not far out. There is a measurable possibility that it is right, so you might want to adjust your position accordingly. On the other hand you may recall having a struggle finding it. It was the first you took and it was very faint.

How good a sight was it? Only you can decide that one, but this is an example of the way you should evaluate your fix.

PRECESSION AND NUTATION

As the years roll on, the stars are creeping slowly to the westward across the celestial sphere. This movement is called *precession* and is generally considered at the same time as another tiny discrepancy to order, *nutation*, which is the name given to the amount that the Earth wobbles on its axis.

The combined effect of these two is that every ten years you need a new Volume 1 of AP 3270. If you have a '2000.0 Epoch' copy and it is 2004, look in the back and you will find a correction on Table 5. You should apply this (it is given in nautical miles and an angular direction) to your star fix to maintain its accuracy. It is also to be used on the PL from a single star being used for a fix against a planet, or some other body. It only concerns stars reduced through Volume 1.

10 Polaris
- the Pole Star

As every schoolboy knows, the Pole Star is located directly over the North Pole, for which it is named. Alone amongst the heavenly bodies it sits apparently still while the whole 'bowl of night' revolves in splendour around it.

Because of its unique situation dead on the Earth's axis, a corrected altitude of Polaris gives, without further ado, the observer's latitude. Long before the Sun's declination was tabulated, Polaris was giving heathen men a yardstick for north/south distance. They didn't know the Earth was round, so they had no idea why it worked. We do, and it works like this.

From the illustration you can see that since the terrestrial horizon is a tangent to the Earth's surface (and hence forms a right angle with the radius which designates the observer's latitude), the altitude of Polaris above this tangent is the same as the angle subtended by the observer's zenith at the centre of the Earth, that is, his latitude.

This works out because the distance to Polaris being effectively infinite, the line joining Polaris to the observer is parallel to the axis of the Earth.

CORRECTIONS TO THE APPARENT ALTITUDE OF POLARIS

Unfortunately, it seems that nothing in the universe is going to give us an even break. Even Polaris wanders from the pole by as much as two degrees. It is therefore necessary to apply some corrections to the apparent altitude (which as always is the sextant altitude corrected for index error and dip).

The first thing to do after correcting the sextant altitude to determine apparent altitude is to make the standard 'star' correction for refraction, as found in the middle column of the bookmark of the almanac (see page 35).

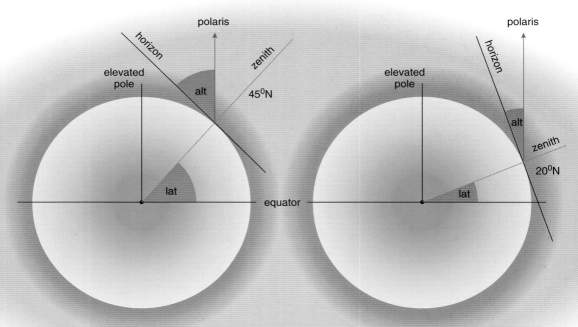

The altitude of Polaris (alt) is virtually the same as the observer's latitude (lat), regardless of whether the navigator is on a latitude of 45⁰N, as on the left, or 20⁰N, as on the right.

Having done this you enter the tables for Polaris immediately before the 'minutes and seconds' increment pages at the back of the almanac. There you will find three corrections: a_0, a_1, and a_2.

For a_0 you enter the tables with your LHA.

For a_1 you enter with your approximate latitude.

For a_2 you simply need to know what month it is.

The only work that you have to do here is solve the LHA of Aries for your approximate position at the time of your sight - to the nearest minute

of time is fine.

In order to keep the arithmetic simple, all the corrections are made positive, but when you have applied them all, you must subtract one degree from the final result to get your latitude. The pro-forma puts all this down in step-by-step form and should remove any doubts you may have about it.

Example

May 1st 1986. DR 51°N 20°W. Polaris is observed during morning twilight at 0552 GMT. Its sextant altitude is 51° 12´.6. Height of eye is 15 feet and index error is 2.8 *off* the arc. What is your latitude?

PRO-FORMA FOR POLARIS

Date	**1 MAY 1986**	
Approximate Latitude:	**51°N**	
DR Long	**20°W**	

Watch time	**05 52**
Correction	**—**
GMT	**05 52**

GHA ♈ (hrs)	**293**	**50.0**
+ Increment (mins/secs)	**13**	**02**
GHA ♈	**306**	**52**
DR Long (approx)	**19**	**52**
LHA ♈	**287**	

Hs	**51**	**21.6**
Index error		**+2.8**
Dip		**-3.8**
Apparent Alt	**51**	**20.6**
Star Correction		**- 0.8**
Ho	**51**	**19.8**
$+a_0$ (LHA♈ **287°**)	**1**	**13.3**
$+a_1$ (Lat **51°N**)		**0.6**
$+a_2$ (month **MAY**)		**0.4**
Sum	**52**	**34.1**
$-1°$		**-1**
LATITUDE	**51° 34´.1 N**	

L.H.A. ARIES	240°– 249°	250°– 259°	260°– 269°	270°– 279°	280°– 289°	290°– 299°	300°– 309°	310°– 319°	320°– 329°
	a_0	a_0	a_0	a_0	a_0	a_0	a_0	a_0	a_0
0	1 41·9	1 37·7	1 32·3	1 25·9	1 18·8	1 11·0	1 02·8	0 54·5	0 46·3
1	41·5	37·2	31·7	25·3	18·0	10·1	01·9	53·6	45·5
2	41·1	36·7	31·1	24·6	17·2	09·3	01·1	52·8	44·7
3	40·7	36·2	30·5	23·9	16·5	08·5	1 00·3	52·0	43·9
4	40·3	35·7	29·9	23·2	15·7	07·7	0 59·4	51·1	43·1
5	1 39·9	1 35·1	1 29·2	1 22·4	1 14·9	1 06·9	0 58·6	0 50·3	0 42·3
6	39·5	34·6	28·6	21·7	14·1	06·1	57·8	49·5	41·5
7	39·1	34·0	28·0	21·0	13·3	05·2	56·9	48·7	40·7
8	38·6	33·5	27·3	20·3	12·6	04·4	56·1	47·9	40·0
9	38·1	32·9	26·6	19·5	11·8	03·6	55·3	47·1	39·2
10	1 37·7	1 32·3	1 25·9	1 18·8	1 11·0	1 02·8	0 54·5	0 46·3	0 38·4

Lat.	a_1	a_1	a_1	a_1	a_1	a_1	a_1	a_1	a_1
0	0·5	0·4	0·4	0·3	0·2	0·2	0·2	0·2	0·3
10	·5	·5	·4	·3	·3	·3	·3	·3	·3
20	·5	·5	·4	·4	·4	·3	·3	·3	·4
30	·5	·5	·5	·4	·4	·4	·4	·4	·4
40	0·6	0·6	0·5	0·5	0·5	0·5	0·5	0·5	0·5
45	·6	·6	·6	·6	·5	·5	·5	·5	·5
50	·6	·6	·6	·6	·6	·6	·6	·6	·6
55	·6	·6	·6	·7	·7	·7	·7	·7	·7
60	·6	·7	·7	·7	·8	·8	·8	·8	·8
62	0·7	0·7	0·7	0·8	0·8	0·8	0·8	0·8	0·8
64	·7	·7	·8	·8	·9	·9	·9	·9	·8
66	·7	·7	·8	·9	0·9	0·9	0·9	0·9	0·9
68	0·7	0·8	0·9	0·9	1·0	1·0	1·0	1·0	1·0

Month	a_2	a_2	a_2	a_2	a_2	a_2	a_2	a_2	a_2
Jan.	0·5	0·5	0·5	0·5	0·5	0·5	0·6	0·6	0·6
Feb.	·4	·4	·4	·4	·4	·4	·4	·4	·5
Mar.	·4	·4	·3	·3	·3	·3	·3	·3	·3
Apr.	0·5	0·4	0·4	0·3	0·3	0·3	0·2	0·2	0·2
May	·6	·6	·5	·4	·4	·3	·3	·2	·2
June	·8	·7	·6	·6	·5	·4	·4	·3	·3
July	0·9	0·8	0·8	0·7	0·7	0·6	0·5	0·5	0·4
Aug.	·9	·9	·9	·8	·8	·8	·7	·6	·6
Sept.	·9	·9	·9	·9	·9	·9	·8	·8	·8
Oct.	0·8	0·8	0·9	0·9	0·9	0·9	0·9	0·9	0·9
Nov.	·6	·7	·8	·8	·9	·9	1·0	1·0	1·0
Dec.	0·5	0·5	0·6	0·7	0·8	0·8	0·9	1·0	1·0

Part of the tables for Polaris from the Nautical Almanac.
The ringed figures are those entered in the example pro-forma.

11 Compass checking on the ocean

When you are out on the ocean the only external means available for checking your compass are those provided by the sky.

It's always worthwhile to know that your deviation card is up-to-date when you are set up on a heading that may, wind permitting, stay more or less constant for days or even weeks. This is how it's done.

SUNSET AND SUNRISE: AMPLITUDE TABLES

Every proprietary nautical almanac should have a page devoted to tables known as amplitude tables. These give the bearing of the Sun in degrees True from your approximate position as it rises or sets.

LAT.	DECLINATION							
	0°	1°	2°	3°	4°	5°	6°	7°
	°	°	°	°	°	°	°	°
0° to 5°	90	89	88	87	86	85	84	83
6°	90	89	88	87	86	85	84	83
7°	90	89	88	87	86	85	84	83
8°	90	89	88	87	86	85	84	82 9
9°	90	89	88	87	86	85	83 9	82 9

A small section of the amplitude tables which give the bearing of the rising or setting Sun. You need to obtain the rough declination of the Sun from the daily pages of the almanac, and an approximate latitude.

If you are able to use your steering compass to take a bearing of the rising Sun, the difference between this and the bearing tabulated will be the total compass error. As you know, compass error is the sum of variation and deviation. Variation in a given area is known from the routeing charts used for ocean passage planning, so once you have applied that to a True bearing what is left can only be deviation.

It's worth noting that while pilot charts will last a lifetime in terms of wind and current, the variation curves they give do alter with the years. In the past, you either replaced them with new ones or turned to another source of up-to-date information on variation. The arrival of GPS receivers with course computers built in has removed this requirement. Most GPS sets will read out a 'course to steer' or 'course made good' in degrees true or degrees magnetic, corrected for zone and annual changes. Even if the read-out will not give the variation as a specific item, it is only necessary to program the instrument to give a course in magnetic, re-jig it to give the same one in true, then compare the two.

Points to note

Because of refraction, the Sun is technically 'rising' or 'setting' when it is one semidiameter

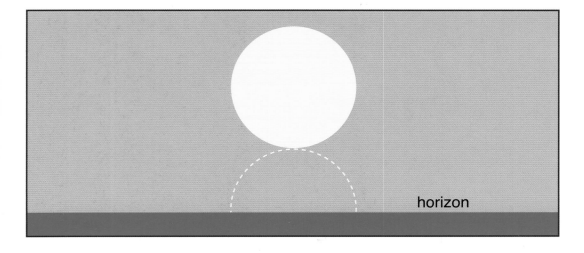

horizon

above the horizon, as in the illustration.

On east-west passages, the Sun often rises or sets on a bearing quite close to your course, either dead ahead or dead astern. If this is almost so, but not quite, a small course alteration to bring it right on the course line will give you its bearing from the steering compass. The difference in deviation between this heading and the course is unlikely to be significant.

If the Sun both sets and rises a large angular distance from your ship's heading then you'll have to measure its bearing relative to the ship's head. By applying that to the compass heading you can deduce its bearing on the steering compass.

The best way of taking the bearing of the setting or rising Sun is by sighting it directly across the steering compass. This is often possible where the instrument is mounted on a binnacle, or is the old-fashioned but ever-green Sestrel compass sited on the coachroof ahead of the cockpit. If you aren't lucky enough to have such an arrangement, you must take a bearing of the Sun relative to the ship's head by some mechanical means. The classic instrument for achieving such a bearing is a pelorus with proper sights and a finely graduated scale, but most yachts do not carry such a thing. However, nearly all use a chart plotter of some description. A workable relative bearing can be taken by setting this up somewhere on deck with zero degrees on the ship's head. You can use the moving arm of the plotter, if it has one, to sight on the Sun. Take some care to 'aim' the arm at the Sun's average position as the boat yaws from side to side of its course. You will have plenty of time to take pains and the results are usually quite satisfactory.

If sea conditions permit, I generally do this every time I'm able to observe the sunrise or the sunset. I enter the results in the back of my log book and maintain a running check on my ship's deviation card. This way any errors produced by using a chart plotter instead of a proper pelorus tend to average out, and any new errors are noticed straightaway.

Example:

Ship's Head by Steering Compass
250°C
Relative bearing of setting Sun
037°
∴ compass Bearing of sun
287°C
Bearing from amplitude tables
283°T
∴ total Compass Error
4°W

But, Variation (from pilot chart or GPS)
7°W
∴ deviation on this heading
3°East

AZIMUTHS FOR COMPASS CHECKS

Another excellent method of using the Sun to check your steering compass when your course is nowhere near the line of the rising or setting Sun is to wait until the Sun is dead ahead or dead astern, note its bearing, and take a sight.

It won't take a moment to work out just the azimuth part of the sight reduction calculation and once you have done so, you have your true ship's heading. You know your compass heading, the chart gives the local variation, so away you go...

12 The shortest way

We all know that the shortest distance from 'A' to 'B' is a straight line. Using a chart produced to the usual Mercator projection, a ruled line connecting two points will indicate a compass heading between them that does not vary. This 'rhumb line' course also represents more or less the least mileage where its length is insignificant compared with the size of the Earth. This feature of Mercator charts is eminently convenient for coastal work. At ocean scales, however, its practicality often breaks down.

Where a course line encompasses a substantial proportion of the globe, the inevitable distortions of the Mercator projection, particularly in higher latitudes, affect routeing to a serious degree.

GREAT CIRCLE SAILING

As we discussed on page 7 of this book, a great circle can be one of the meridians of longitude which converge at the poles but, apart from

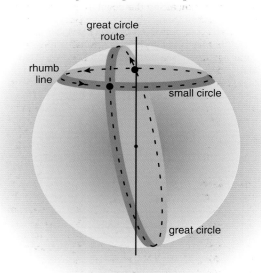

Right and above: On a Mercator chart a great circle route near the pole appears as a curved line, longer than the rhumb line. But if you look at the two routes as they appear on the globe, it is obvious that the great circle route is shorter.

the equator, no parallel of latitude fits the description. A great circle, however, does not have to be one of these two. It is in fact any line depicted on the surface of the Earth by a plane which passes through its centre. The shortest distance between two points on the surface of a sphere is always the track of the great circle on which both are situated. When deciding which course to steer from one side of an ocean to the other, this is one of the factors you should consider.

Were you to sail a rhumb line on the Mercator projection of your chosen ocean, you will end up by travelling a more or less greater distance than you need have done, depending upon your latitude and how closely your course approaches due east or due west.

In high latitudes, on east-west headings, the rhumb line diverges substantially from the great circle route, while on similar headings on the equator (itself a great circle), they are one and the same. In any latitude a heading of due north or south is, by definition, a great circle, but as your headings swing away from this, the differences begin to compound.

In practice, if you are crossing the North Atlantic from Cape Race to the Bishop Rock and you are able to steer your desired course all the way, you will save several hundred miles by operating on the great circle. If you are crossing in the trades from the Cape Verdes to the Caribbean, any savings on the great circle track will be much smaller and will almost certainly be overshadowed by other considerations.

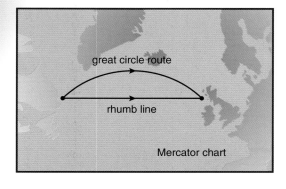

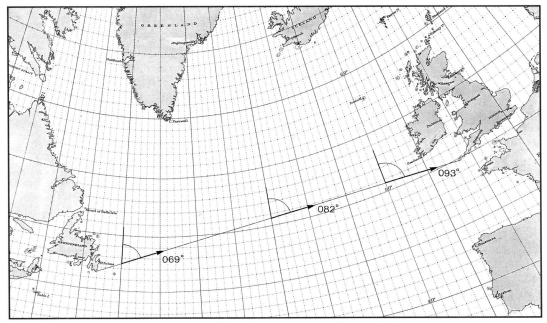

A great circle route from Cape Race to the Bishop Rock, plotted on a Gnomonic chart.

Working the Great Circle

Fortunately for the non-mathematical ocean navigator, charts covering all major routes are available upon which a straight line is, in fact, a great circle. This happy property of the Gnomonic projection makes planning a great circle route the simplest of tasks.

The illustration shows a Gnomonic chart of the North Atlantic, with the great circle route from Cape Race to the Bishop Rock drawn in. You will notice that it crosses each of the converging meridians at a slightly different angle. To determine the course at any particular meridian, you place your plotter north and south at the line of longitude and read off the course. Although ideally the course should change at each meridian, in practice you travel five or ten degrees and then lay off the next heading, proceeding in a series of rhumb lines from one great circle point to the next.

To lift a course from a Gnomonic chart you will need a plotter of the 'Breton' type or a small Douglas protractor. Parallel rules will be of little use. Lay the north-south line of the plotter grid along the charted meridian at your position, and read off the course from a light line plotted from it to the destination.

Navigators of steamers and motor yachts are advised to lift a series of points from their Gnomonic chart and pre-plot them onto a Mercator projection for day-to-day navigation purposes. The results look like the diagram on page 62. This is not recommended for sailing craft because the nature of ocean weather generally dictates the detail of their tracks. As with navigation along the coast, it is rarely worth plotting a line along which you expect to travel, because however carefully you may plan a great-circle route, if you are in a sailing vessel I would stake a case of rum to a can of beer that you will not follow it.

A hundred miles out you will experience either a headwind or, in the trades, a wind that puts you onto a dead run. In neither case will you steer your course any more and all your planning will have been blown to bits.

What you actually do is this: Set out on a great circle with hope in your heart, but at all times sail your ship so as to travel as fast as sensibly possible in the most achievable comfort. Soon you'll be miles from your hoped-for track. Ocean navigation, like all navigation, consists of estimating or fixing your position and then shaping the best course you can from there to your destination. So after you have produced a decent fix and plotted it onto your Mercator chart, you then whip out your Gnomonic projection and pop it on there as well. Now lay off a new great circle heading. If you are lucky this one will last you more than a couple of days, but the sea and fore-and-aft rig being what they are, it probably won't.......

GPS and the Great Circle

An interesting development in great circle sailing which is a by-product of the GPS package is that the inbuilt course computer will automatically give you a course from your current position to your destination. All you have to do is punch in an arrival waypoint. At any time you need only press the 'go to' button and the computer will read out the distance and course to steer which, on most machines, will be a great circle. This theoretically renders the Gnomonic chart redundant but, for an old-fashioned chap like me, it's still reassuring to actually see the great circle laid out as a straight line across that weird grid.

COMPOSITE TRACKS

There can be any number of reasons why a pure great circle may take you to unacceptable places. Perhaps it skirts too closely unlit, isolated dangers. Maybe it goes too far towards the pole and the iceberg menace for your fancy, or perchance it is leading you into an area notorious for its lack of breeze. If any of these is the case, the usual solution is to follow the great-circle track until you arrive at the parallel of latitude which you have decided will delimit the danger, run east or west along it until the great circle re-emerges from the danger area and then join it once more to continue to your destination.

A classic example of this is a vessel running her easting down in the Southern Ocean with nearly half the globe to traverse. The great circle would pass far too close to the ice, so it is up to the skipper to decide by how much he wants to clear this hazard. When the chosen latitude is reached, course is altered to run as nearly as possible along the parallel. As soon as the great circle veers off towards the safe side of the danger zone, the yacht can re-join it.

Great circle sailing may only make a small difference in the Tropics, but the conscientious application of these principles as you sail the oceans in mid or high latitudes can save literally days. Every little helps when you are out there and, as Norie's definition of navigation points out, we must conduct our ships not only with 'the greatest safety' from one part of the ocean to another, but also 'in the shortest time possible'.

PRO-FORMA FOR SUN SIGHT

Date _____

Watch time
Correction
GMT

GHA (hrs)
+Correction (mins/secs)
GHA
Assumed Long   Assumed Lat _____
LHA

Hc		z		Declination (hrs)	
d		180/360		d difference	
Hc		Zn		Declination	

Hs
Index Error
Dip
Apparent Alt
Main Correction
Ho
Hc
Intercept   TOWARDS/AWAY

A standard sunsight proforma. Together with shooting the Sun on your meridian for latitude, this is the most important sight you will take day by day. Understand this proforma and the others are simply a question of detail.